HANDBOOK
FOR A
DISCIPLE OF JESUS

Unless otherwise indicated, all scripture quotations are taken from the New King James Version of the Bible.
Distributed by: TheBibleForYou.com

CONTENTS

Preface	
Introduction	1
Who Are You?	8
The Price of the Sin-Nature	14
A Prayer of Salvation	15
I. What is the New Testament	16
Grace Replaces the Old Law	16
Eternally Saved through ONE Sacrifice: Jesus	18
Being Born Again	19
Our New Identity in Christ	21
The Power of Declarations	23
The Boldness of Righteousness	25
II. God's Gift to New Believers: The Holy Spirit	30
The Spirit of Truth and the Power of God	30
The Gift of Tongues	32
Hearing from God	34
III. The Living Word of God	36
Jesus is the Word of God ~ The Creator	39
God's Word cannot Fail	40
The <u>Benefits</u> of knowing God's Word	41
Study and Meditate on God's Word	43
Obedience is the Key~Faith without Works is Dead	44
Memorization of the Word	45
IV. Living a Vibrant Relationship with God	
is the Essence of the New Testament	47
The Believer's Relationship with the Lord	47
How much God Loves Us	48
Faith ~ the Only Way to Please God	50
Enduring Faith ~ God's Waiting Room	52
Believers are Given the Full Authority of Christ	56
Honoring the Lord in all of Our Ways	57
Resting in the Lord ~ The True Sabbath	58
V. PRAYER: The Believer's Direct Line to God	61
God Hears and Answers Every Prayer	62
Pray in Faith, Fully Believing	65
Praising and Worshiping God	66

VI. Discipleship Means "Walking Out" Your Faith	69
What it Means to be a Christian Disciple	69
Christians must Bear Fruit	73
The Christian's Relationship to the World	75
A Surrendered Life (Not My Will)	79
Raising Children is "Discipling"	80
VII. Winning the Spiritual Warfare	84
The War is in the Mind~Renewing the Mind	85
How to be "More than Conquerors"	89
Be "On Guard"	91
VIII. Freely You Have Received, Freely Give	95
Jesus Healed ALL that were Sick	96
Authority to Heal the Sick, Cast out Demons, Raise the Dead, Cleanse the Lepers	98
YOU can be Healed Too!	99
IX. Religiosity vs Christianity	102
The "Sacred Cows" of Religion	105
Beware of Self-Righteousness	107
Persecution for Christ's Sake	108
X. Witnessing Our Faith	112
The Great Commission	112
Unashamed Boldness and Conviction	116
Manifesting a True Christian Life	117
The Christian's Love for the World	117
Let's keep Our Witness Simple	121
Unity amongst Believers	122
Walking in Humility	124
XI. Finances of the Kingdom	129
Promises of Blessings	131
Stewardship and Integrity	134
Giving	137
XII. The Power of Our Words	140
Authority Through Spoken Words	140
The Uncontrolled Mouth	142
Power of the Spoken Word	142
Anger and Strife	142
Gossiping and Lying	145
Judging and Criticizing	145

Bitterness vs Forgiveness	146
Kind Words and Encouragement	148
XIII. Powerful Promises of God in Times of Difficulties	150
Peace that Passes all Understanding	151
Do not Fear	154
Claim God's Protection	156
Depend on His Strength and Power	160
God Promises Comfort in Tribulation	163
Get His Wisdom and Knowledge	164
XIV. Creation vs. Evolution	167
XV. The End of Time	171
The Signs of the Endtime	172
XVI. Memory Verses	178
What is the New Testament?	178
God's Gift to New Believers: The Holy Spirit	178
The Living Word of God	179
Living a Vibrant Relationship with God is the New Testament	179
PRAYER: The Believer's Direct Line to God	180
Religiosity vs Christianity	182
Witnessing Your Faith	183
Finances of the Kingdom	184
The Power of Our Words	185
Powerful Promises of God in Times of Difficulties	185
Other Special Verses	186
The End of Time Verses the Last Days	186
Chapters and Passages	187

PREFACE

The purpose of *The Handbook for a Disciple of Jesus* is to clearly outline the basic beliefs that form the foundation of true biblical Christianity. We have selected many scriptures that a disciple of Jesus should build his life on, and have categorized them for easy reference. Jesus said, *"The Words that I speak unto you, they are Spirit and they are life" (John 6:63)*. Our goal is to impart these powerful words of life to you!

Our stance of faith in Christ cannot be "ho hum", and indifferent. True Christianity is fervent, engaged and dedicated. Lukewarmness should have no place in the heart of a disciple of Jesus. There is no such thing as the peaceful coexistence of good and evil. Jesus said, *"He who is not with Me is against Me: and he who does not gather with Me scatters" (Lk.11:23)*. This is the position that a disciple should take from the start. Once we've <u>seen</u> the light and have been given the opportunity to be a light to the world, why should we ever choose darkness again or <u>be</u> "on the fence" about following Him?

While there are many teachers in the body of Christ, the very best teacher is Jesus Himself and the actual Word of God, the Bible. Our goal as Christians is to walk out the standard of <u>discipleship</u> that Jesus gave to those who will "follow after Him".

You could consider this handbook as a condensed <u>discipleship course</u>. Once you have read through this whole handbook, and absorbed its teachings and instructions, you will know the basics that you need to know in order to understand the Bible as well as to win people to Jesus, heal the sick, cast out demons, make disciples and set up Bible groups. All this, for as long as you are a DOER of the Word, not a hearer only.

This handbook should be used as a pocket companion for all disciples of Jesus who want to live in the Word and establish a firm foundation of faith. Carry it with you so that you have those verses at your fingertips whenever you witness, or need some power for the hour for yourself. As you read and meditate on these scriptures, they will be a continual source of strength and direction for your own life, and a great tool to instruct and teach others.

If you're a teacher of the Word, each one of these sections can be developed into a Bible class by simply unwrapping and teaching on each of the verses in the different sections. At the beginning of most sections, we have added a text to keynote these Bible verses. However, as you read these scriptures, His Spirit will teach you, and *"lead you into all truth."* (Jn 16:13).

Note: At the end of this handbook in the "Memorization" section is a list of many important verses that every Christian should know and be well acquainted with. You could either memorize them or review them regularly. All of these verses are the core scriptures of each of the basic beliefs of the Christian faith. You'll easily find them in the different sections of this handbook because they are all marked with an asterisk (*) in the margin.

Also, there is a "review system" at the end of the that will help you revisit those same verses on a regular basis so you won't forget them. Remember, the more verses we know deep in our hearts, the more powerful our prayer life and our witness will be.

INTRODUCTION

Dream Big- Faith It!

Before we go into it, we want to keynote this handbook by saying that the life of a Christian has to first be a life of unrestrained faith. –Meaning that we must not only believe, but put our full trust in something bigger than ourselves–God.

Christians are to dream!–and dream big! That's really what faith is. God wants us to be all, and do all that He has for us in our life! He wants us to live a full life and to live courageously. He told Joshua, *"Fear not, be bold" (Josh 1:9)*. Fear of failure is the beginning of failing, but courage is moving forward in spite of fear. Others say it's impossible, but *"all things are possible to him that believes" (Mat 9:29)*. Jesus had a very different approach to impossibilities. He said, *"With men it is impossible, but not with God; for with God all things are possible" (Mk 10:27)*.

There are laws that God established in our world, and they work all the time, for anyone and everyone, and they work everywhere, regardless of where you live in this world. They are oftentimes referred to as "universal laws". The law of gravity is one of those, but there are many more.

The science of quantum physics is discovering many of those laws, and proving them to be true, and how we are all affected by those laws. Another important law is *"as a man thinks in his heart, so is he" (Pro 23:7)*. We become what we magnify in our hearts, and what we mostly focus on (Rom 6:16).

Many of those laws are outlined in the Proverbs of Solomon, and of course Jesus explained many of them in His teachings. The parable of the sower for instance explains how the whole world operates on the power of a seed and the fertility of our heart. And He compares the seed to the Word of God and how it can create an awesome harvest in our life. There are many parables where Jesus started by saying, "The Kingdom of God is as…." and He explains yet another law of the universe. That is why the Bible is so powerful; more so than any other book;

because, therein are all those laws and principles of how our world operates and how we're supposed to pattern our lives, so that we live happy, productive and fulfilling lives.

Another one of those laws is that our own words are also seeds. And they carry either life or death. They carry BLESSINGS or curses. Therefore whatever we say affects us and consequently our path in life. People who always have something bad to say about their job, their personal situation, etc., end up reaping exactly what they sow through their words. Again, it's a law of the universe. It works for the just and the unjust; and it works for good and for bad. It works with our thoughts as well. People who constantly worry call down troubles into their lives. People who fear sickness end up causing sickness to take root in their body simply by focusing so much attention on it. The power of faith works the same way. You can believe for great things to come into your life and your very expectations and imagination will call those blessings to you.

The world system will try to mold you ; in fact, tests and trials in life will mold you. Life in general will change you one way or the other. But we can actually choose the mold we're forced into. We can choose to be molded by God's loving hand, the potter's hand, to mold the vessel of our life. The Word of God says, *"Do not be conformed to this world, but be transformed by the renewing of your mind, that you may prove what is that good and acceptable and perfect will of God" (Ro 12:1)*. Let the promises of God take you as far as you can go in fulfilling the destiny that He has designed just for you.

Perhaps it is true that we're programmed for failure by the world, but we're wired for success by God if only we'll follow Him. Eph 3:20 says, *"Now to Him who is able to do exceedingly abundantly above all that we ask or think, according to the power that works in us"*. Dreaming is very much akin to faith; ever believing above the circumstances of life. Dreaming big will provide a ladder to your goals and visions. We must never stop dreaming even when our dreams are shattered, because our dreams are a constant glimpse into our destiny. The Word says, *"Therefore do not cast away your confidence, which has great reward. For you have the need of endurance, so that after you have done the will of God, you may receive the promise" (Heb 10:35,36).*

Joseph of old was a dreamer and he was ridiculed and persecuted by his brothers because of it, but he was willing to endure controversy in order to remain faithful to his dream. All through his life, even though he went through so many tests, he kept an excellent spirit because he stayed faith-full to God.

Jesus defines greatness in Mat 23:11. *"Let the greatest among you be the servant of all. For whoever makes himself great shall be humbled and whoever humbles himself shall be made great"*. One who is great, according to the Bible, is one who is humble in spirit and is a servant of all. That's what makes you great; your willingness to serve others. That's how Joseph was blessed by God. He was a servant with an excellent spirit in Potiphar's house, in jail, and even as the right-hand man of the pharaoh.

For God to bless our dreams, we must understand the need to love, share and give. The greatest fulfilment in life is to share and contribute towards helping others. We're not to live for ourselves. The pursuit of "bigger barns" for our own benefit leads only to more stress, more fear, and more dissatisfaction. But God is eager to bless all those who share and give. *"Every good and perfect gift comes from God" (Jam 1:17)*. It's when we finally realize that all that we receive is from Him, that we're free to share and to give abundantly. That's how we can walk humbly and serve others; not to center our whole life around ourselves. That doesn't work. It must be what Jesus meant when He said, *"lose your life for My sake and you will find it" (Mat 10:39)*.

The Bible says that we become the slave of our domineering thoughts (Rom 6:16). We become the result of what we focus our thoughts on and commit to. Whatever we are most passionate about, is what we become. That basically means that we must guard our thoughts to stay committed to our faith and to our dream. Or else, if we don't commit to anything we become nothing. A dream without goals is just fantasizing and daydreaming. Great people of God are people, like you and me, who made an extraordinary commitment to a cause greater than themselves. The Apostle Paul said, *"But one thing I do, forgetting those things which are behind and reaching forward to those things which are ahead, I press toward the goal for the prize of the upward call of God in Christ Jesus" (Phil 3:13,14).*

To have a dream, is more than a simple wish. It is a deep craving, an intense longing. Dreaming is an excitement in the inner man. It is an intense desire that takes lukewarmness out of life. Dreaming is not plaintive and beggarly. It is filled with passion and assurance. Two things are intolerable to God: insincerity (Mt 23:28) and lukewarmness (Rev 3:16); lack of heart and lack of heat.

It is the people who refuse to quit that make it to the finish line. Your carnal mind will fight your dreams, but we must listen to our heart. God has a plan for all of us–a destiny of integrity and excellence. *"For I know the thoughts that I think toward you, says the Lord, thoughts of peace and not of evil, to give you a future and a hope" (Jer 29:11-13).* We limit God in our thoughts because the mind sees the impossibilities. But God is a God of possibilities. God has given us a powerful mind and we are capable of doing anything, because we *"can do all things through Christ" (Phil 4:13).*

But there's a price to pay. We must learn to *"lay aside every weight, and the sin which so easily ensnares us, and let us run with endurance the race that is set before us" (Heb 12:2).* We must learn to let go of the things that will not matter in the end. We must look past the pain to the payoff. *"Delight yourself also in the Lord, and He shall give you the desires of your heart"* (Ps 37:4). *"He shall bring forth your righteousness as the light, and your justice as the noonday" (Ps 37:4,6).* That is the power that faith has. We can believe beyond our feelings because God has given man the ability to visualize things that are not (yet).

Our imagination is one of the strongest weapons we have because it's an image maker. We must learn to use our imagination to meditate on the things of God. In other words, in focusing on the promises of God, we make our feelings obey the destiny God has for us in His Word. Meditation is a desire to absorb and to receive to the point of becoming; it's not mere observation, it's a discipline of change. We must visualize ourselves succeeding on the inside before we can see it on the outside. We can understand deep thoughts if we meditate on them and imagine them in our heart. Actually, we can't move any further in life until we visualize ourselves there. You will not give birth to what is inside of you until you conceive it in your imagination; you have to see yourself healed before you can be healed, you have to see yourself prosperous before you can reach your success. And when we speak the Word aloud to ourselves, it brings what's on the inside of us to reality on the outside. There's something about the vibration of our voice that has creative power when we speak out your faith. "Faith comes by hearing" (Rom 10:17).

The ability to visualize a scripture into a picture makes it come from the spiritual to the physical. Through meditation on God's Word, you can literally bring every thought into the reality of what Christ says about you and your potential. Meditation is positive 'worry', if you may. The same part of you that worries is the part of you that meditates. Keep your mind stayed on God's Word and see yourself succeeding.

Read and re-read Psalm 1 to yourself regularly. Let the sponge of your imagination soak in as much Word as possible and visualize the change in you; you will then be able to refute all evil imaginations trying to come inside of you. That is why the Bible says that we must *"keep all of our thoughts into captivity, to the obedience of Christ" (1 Cor 10:5)*. The Word says, *"If you observe lying vanities, you forsake your own mercies" (Jonah 2:8)*. So let the Word of God release its life inside of you. It's a seed that you plant in your heart, and watered by your faith, by and by it takes root. (See the parable of the sower – Mat 13.)

God wants us to live courageously and victoriously. If we live in fear we live a small life, because fear causes us to stop and do nothing; the more we rehearse our problems, the bigger they will grow. Fear prevents forward progress. We fear criticism, exposure, the unknown, etc. Send faith to answer when they come to your door. Rehearse the promises and the possibilities of God for your life.

Our brain was not made for negativity, nor can it handle it. The Word says, *"Fix your thoughts on what is true, and honorable, and right, and pure, and lovely, and admirable. Think about things that are excellent and worthy of praise"* (Phil 4:8) and discipline your mind <u>not</u> to think otherwise.

If you want to know God's will for your life, stick your nose in His Word every single day. Make it your top priority to spend time with God every day. God wants to be at the center of your life; not just a part, not the extra bits, but the nucleus. *"In all your ways acknowledge Him, and He shall direct your paths" (Pr 3:6).*

Remember, you will center your life on something. If it's not God, it'll be some idol that will lead you astray and into living an unfruitful life. Nothing else but God's Word is strong enough to hold you and your dream together. *"Commit your works to the Lord, and your thoughts will be established" (Pr 16:3).*

The Word of God will make you smart, smarter than your teachers. *"I have more understanding than all my teachers, for Your testimonies are my meditation" (Ps 119:99).* His Word is alive and powerful and will lift your life into a destiny that you never could have dreamed of. Read Psalm 119 regularly in order to understand the full power of God's Word in your life.

God is all powerful for you. Nothing is impossible to you. Abide in Him and then *"ask and you shall receive" (Jn 15:7).* Discipline your life to the study of the Word and be consistent and give it all you've got. Be all in, and persevere. Perseverance is faith under endurance. Jesus told Peter, *"I have prayed for you, that your faith should not fail" (Lk 22:32).*

Remember you won't go through life alone, not in your name alone, but in Jesus's name, filled with His Spirit. He's given us the power of attorney to use His name. This means you can face obstacles using His credit card, if you may; using His power and His authority. It's all in the new contract created through the power of the Cross.

So let's not limit God by our small thinking (Ps 78:41). Read His Word and dig out those universal laws created for you. This handbook was created to help you discover those laws that will work for you. Remember they're laws of God and they work always, all ways.

Just dare to trust God and not your own strength, but *"trust in the Lord always"(Pro 3:5)*. Don't trust in your war horse (your own abilities) to give you victory (Ps 33:17,18). Regardless of how weak or how old you are, you can still make the rest of your life the best of your life.

Christianity is not a comfortable life, it is a classroom towards the greater goal of life; to learn unselfishness. The whole Bible can be condensed into two sentences: *"Love the Lord your God with all your heart"* and *"love your neighbor as yourself" (Mk 12:30,31)*. We find our life by losing it, for the benefit of God and others (Jn 12:24; Lk 9:23). All the trials of life are to teach us to live unselfishly and be more like Jesus (Ro 8:28). A life of giving and loving.

We were made in love by a God of love and are meant to live a life of love, for love, through love, and in love in order to give love. Nothing else will be as fulfilling. So why settle for less. Remain a student, a learner and a doer of the discipline of Christ, your whole life.

Don't fake it, faith it, and DREAM BIG.

WHO ARE YOU?

God originally created man after His own image (Gen 1:26-28). And the first commandment that God gave to Adam was to have dominion over the whole earth, and to subdue it and to govern it. God crowned man the prince of this world and it is only through the disobedience of Adam that Satan stole that title, and took his authority and became the prince of the world, and because of that, sin and death entered into the world (2Cor 4:4). *"Therefore, just as through one man sin entered the world, and death through sin, and thus death spread to all men, because all sinned"* (Rom 5:12). This was not an instant physical death, but it was a spiritual death. Spiritual death actually means separation from God.

The Bible says that the devil is a liar from the beginning. *"He was a murderer from the beginning, and does not stand in the truth, because there is no truth in him. When he speaks a lie, he speaks from his own resources, for he is a liar and the father of it"* (John 8:44). Therefore, after the fall of Adam, all men were born into sin. *"He who sins is of the devil, for the devil has sinned from the beginning. For this purpose the Son of God was manifested, that He might destroy the works of the devil"* (1 John 3:8). This verse explains why Jesus came to redeem man from his sin nature.

Through His sacrifice, Jesus won the dominion back from the devil. *"Who Himself bore our sins in His own body on the tree, that we, having died to sins, might live for righteousness—by whose stripes you were healed"* (1 Pet 2:24). *"And Jesus came and spoke to them, saying, 'All authority has been given to Me in heaven and on earth"* (Mat 28:18). The devil was not destroyed, but his dominion and rule over man and over the earth was destroyed. For Christians this is the most important fact to acknowledge in the New Testament, otherwise we are going to think that we are still under the enemy's oppression and power.

Jesus bridged the gap between God and man by conquering sin. *"For He made Him who knew no sin to be sin for us, that we might become the righteousness of God in Him"* (2Cor 5:21). Remember, the spiritual death of Adam meant separation from

God. But Jesus reconciled man to God through His sacrifice on the cross *(Ro 5:10)*.

This is a very important point to understand. Through faith in the sacrifice of Jesus, man can now be back in full relationship with his Father. *"Which He worked in Christ when He raised Him from the dead and seated Him at His right hand in the heavenly places, far above all principality and power and might and dominion, and every name that is named, not only in this age but also in that which is to come. And He put all things under His feet, and gave Him to be head over all things to the church" (Eph 1:20 - 22)*. God has positioned Jesus above ALL. He is the head and we are His body; we're not separate. We are ONE and therefore we are in the same position of authority. The enemy has been unarmed from all authority and dominion.

God made a promise of BLESSING to Abraham in Deuteronomy 28. And that promise has now been passed on to us through the sacrifice of Jesus Christ. *"That the blessing of Abraham might come upon the gentiles in Christ Jesus, that we might receive the promise of the Spirit through faith" (Gal 3:14)*. Jesus was the first partaker of the Spirit! Then to all who believe in Him after the day of Pentecost; and what is the Holy Spirit for? It is given for miraculous power to witness, and to bring the kingdom of God on earth as it is in heaven. *"For you are all sons of God through faith in Christ Jesus. For as many of you as were baptized into Christ have put on Christ. And if you are Christ's, then you are Abraham's seed, and heirs according to the promise" (Gal 3:26, 27, 29)*. This means that we are heirs of the promise of the Spirit just like Christ was and is! So as heirs, we got what He got! And therefore we should be able to do what He did!

Since we are heirs by what Jesus did for us, we get the same inheritance as Jesus! *"But when the fullness of the time had come, God sent forth His Son, born of a woman, born under the law, to redeem those who were under the law, that we might receive the adoption as sons. And because you are sons, God has sent forth the Spirit of His Son into your hearts, crying out, "Abba, Father!" Therefore, you are no longer a slave but a son, and if a son, then an heir of God through Christ" (Gal 4:4-7)*.

Again, this is so important to understand. That we are actually <u>joint heirs with Christ</u>. That means that we have the same power to set the captives free from all oppressions of the devil. Joint heirs means that we get the full inheritance, one hundred percent of whatever He has. Not only part of it.

However, we are to grow up to be conformed to the same exact image of Christ in this world. Not in the world to come. HERE and now is when we need the POWER, not in the world to come. *"Love has been perfected among us in this: that we may have boldness in the Day of Judgment; because as He is, so are <u>we in this world</u>" (1 John 4:17)*. *"For in Him dwells all the fullness of the Godhead bodily; and you are <u>complete in Him</u>, who is the head of all principality and power" (Col 2:9, 10)*.

So realizing who we are in Christ and the power that has been given us is <u>the key</u> to us understanding the life that Jesus intended for us to live as His followers. Not only are we complete in Him, but we are also empowered by His Spirit to do what He has done.

Paul, the apostle was preaching in all of his epistles about the revelation that He received from Jesus about the "mystery" of the gospel. *"To them God willed to make known what are the riches of the glory of this <u>mystery</u> among the gentiles: which is <u>Christ in you</u>, the hope of glory" (Col 1:27)*. He said: *"How that by revelation He made known to me the mystery (as I have briefly written already, by which, when you read, you may understand my knowledge in the mystery of Christ), which in other ages was not made known to the sons of men, as it has now been revealed by the Spirit to His holy apostles and prophets: that the Gentiles should be <u>fellow heirs</u>, of the same body, and partakers of His promise in Christ through the gospel" (Eph 3:3- 6)*.

Most Christians understand that at the new birth, Jesus comes to live in their heart, and consequently they have eternal life. However, to understand the <u>true depth</u> of what was done at the new birth, is not something that most Christians fully grasp. Jesus not only lives in us, God's Spirit dwells in us and Jesus has given us <u>His name and His authority to use</u> as we will . And therefore all principalities and powers are subjugated to us. We are His body and He the head. We are <u>one</u> as He is one in the Father.

This is exactly what Jesus explained to the believers who followed Him. *"And He said to them, 'Go into all the world and preach the gospel to every creature. He who believes and is baptized will be saved; but he who does not believe will be condemned. And these signs will follow <u>those who believe</u>: In My name they will cast out demons; they will speak with new tongues; they will take up serpents; and if they drink anything deadly thing, it will by no means hurt them; they will lay hands on the sick, and they will recover.'"* *"So then, after the Lord had spoken to them, He was received up into heaven, and sat down at the right hand of God. And <u>they went out and preached</u> everywhere, the Lord working with them and confirming the word through the accompanying signs" (Mk 16: 15- 20)*. So this means that <u>any</u> believer can and should be <u>manifesting</u> these signs and miracles! Notice that Jesus did not tell them to PRAY for the sick. He said, *"Heal the sick, cleanse the lepers, and raise the dead, cast out devils."* These are all authoritative <u>commands</u>.

Jesus said: *"<u>All authority</u> has been given to Me in heaven and on earth. Go therefore and <u>make disciples</u> of all the nations, baptizing them in the name of the Father and of the Son and of the Holy Spirit" (Matthew 28:18, 19)*. So if Jesus has ALL power, that means the devil has NONE. And if Jesus commanded us to walk as He walked (1 Jn 2:6), then it must be possible for us to <u>do</u> the <u>same things</u> He did. *"Most assuredly, I say to you, he who believes in Me, the works that I do he will do also; and greater works than these he will do, because I go to My Father" (John 14:12)*.

Jesus <u>reclaimed dominion</u> over the earth and gave it back to <u>believers</u> along with the authority to subjugate the devil, and He promised to send us the power of the Holy Spirit to help us. *"But you shall receive power when the Holy Spirit has come upon you; and you shall be witnesses to Me in Jerusalem, and in all Judea and Samaria, and to the end of the earth" (Ac 1:8)*. The power of the Holy Spirit is miraculous power. *"Therefore, if anyone is in Christ, he is a new creation; old things have passed away; behold, all things have become new. Now all things are of God, who has reconciled us to Himself through Jesus Christ, and has given us the ministry of reconciliation" (2 Cor 5:17, 18).*

This means that the same ministry of reconciling all things unto God has been given to us. Along with the authority, the power and the name of Jesus to do it with. But the key words are to <u>DO IT</u>. It's not enough to know about it, or to hear about it. This is why Jesus kept insisting on being <u>DOERS</u> of His Word and not hearers only, thus deceiving ourselves. Jesus made a very clear distinction between HEARING and DOING. He said, *"Therefore, whoever hears these sayings of Mine, and <u>DOES</u> them, I will liken him to a <u>WISE MAN</u> who built his house on the <u>ROCK</u>: and the rain descended, the floods came, and the winds blew and beat on that house; and it did <u>NOT fall</u>, for it was founded on the <u>rock</u>. But everyone who hears these sayings of Mine, and <u>DOES NOT</u> do them, will be like a <u>FOOLISH MAN</u> who built his house on the SAND and the rain descended, the floods came, and the winds blew and beat on that house; and it fell. And GREAT was its fall." (Mat 7:24-27).*

In other words, the DOING is the most important part of the Christian life. How much like the devil to blind Christians into believing that if only they hear the Word, it'll be sufficient. But not so! We were predestined by God, before the foundation of the world, to rule here on this earth, to take care of the works of His hands, to <u>replenish</u> the earth with His image (make disciples of all nations), to subdue the earth (by destroying the works of the devil) and have dominion over all things.

This is what Jesus paid a mighty price for. To bring not only man, but the earth back into full reconciliation to God. This is why Paul was so adamant in teaching. *"That the God of our Lord Jesus Christ, the Father of glory, may give to you the spirit of wisdom and revelation in the knowledge of Him, <u>the eyes</u> of your understanding being <u>enlightened</u>; (opened), that you may know what is the hope of His calling, what are the <u>riches</u> of the glory of His <u>inheritance</u> in the saints, and what is the exceeding greatness of His power toward us <u>who believe</u>, according to the working of His mighty power which He worked in Christ when He raised Him from the dead and seated Him at His right hand in the* *heavenly places, <u>far above all principality and power and might</u> and dominion, and every name that is named, not only in this age but also in that which is to come. And He put all things under His feet, and gave Him to be head <u>over all things</u> to the church, which is <u>His body</u>, the fullness of Him who fills all in all." (Eph 1:17 - 23).*

So for all who desire to be disciples of Jesus, let this be the <u>ruling principle</u> before reading His Word. We must understand <u>who we are in Christ</u> and the power that He has given to us through the redemption of the cross. We have been given the <u>keys of the kingdom</u>, which is to <u>bind and to lose</u> on earth and to know that heaven will back us up accordingly. We have the full power and authority in us through His name, IF we will <u>DO IT</u>.

THE PRICE OF THE SIN-NATURE

Jesus paid a high price on the cross to redeem us from the "sin nature" that we were all born with. The sin nature is what separated us from God. Because of Adam and Eve's sin, or what is called the 'fall of man', we are all born in sin; separated from our Father.

This sinful nature is not fully understood by most people before they are "born again". In fact, many believe that a sinful lifestyle is normal. Just look at most TV shows, social media memes, and movies. They employ "sinful" attitudes and lifestyles for humor, normalcy and horror. Rarely in the media do you see the consequences of sin. Satan disguises sin to make it look attractive, desirable, normal and needful.

However, sin has all sorts of negative consequences in our lives: guilt, shame, stress, fear, confusion, worry, insecurity and many physical and emotional illnesses and troubles, all of which can lead to self-condemnation, isolation, depression and even death. King David said, *"For my iniquities have gone over my head; Like a heavy burden they are too heavy for me" (Psalm 38:4)*. The devil first tempts you to sin and then condemns you for sinning. He comes only to *"steal, kill and destroy" (Jn 10:10)*, but Jesus came to bring us life. *"I am come that they might have life, and that they might have it more abundantly." (Jn 10:10)*.

Man was originally created to live in harmony with his Creator. God made us and He loves us! And He paid the highest price of sacrificing His own Son to die for us, so that we could come back to Him and live in harmony with Him!

The Bible says, *"For by grace you have been saved through faith, and that not of yourselves; it is the gift of God, not of works, lest anyone should boast." (Eph 2:8-9)*. Man can't save himself, not by good works and not by self-improvement. Only through accepting the sacrifice of Jesus can we be reunited to God. It's God's most precious gift of grace to man.

If you're ready to be born again, pray this prayer:

A PRAYER OF SALVATION

"Dear Jesus, I don't want my sin nature to separate me from You any longer. You have promised that if I confess my sins, repent and ask for forgiveness, that I will be forgiven for everything that I have done wrong. I believe in You, and in the sacrifice You've made to redeem me, by dying in my stead. And I believe that You rose again to reunite me with the Father.

"I trust You when You say salvation comes by grace, through faith, and not by anything I do. I receive You into my life as my Lord, my Savior. And I want my life transformed by Your Word and Your Holy Spirit. So I'm turning over every part of my life to You.

"I want to live the way You created me to live, for the rest of my life. I want to get to know You and learn to love You and learn of Your love for me and others.

"I ask You to save me and accept me into Your family.

"In Jesus' name I pray. Amen."

I. WHAT IS THE NEW TESTAMENT

There is a huge difference between the old and the new testaments in the Bible. That blank page separates an <u>old</u> contract and covenant between God and man, and it opens up to a <u>new</u> covenant established through the sacrifice that Jesus made by giving His life to <u>redeem mankind</u> and bring us back into fellowship with God.

In the new testament, Jesus, as the Son of God, came as a man to repossess that which was lost, which is our identity and our image, made after the image of God. His purpose was to redeem us of the sin nature (rebellion) that the enemy brought in through the fall of Adam. God's grace paid the price for the full redemption of all of man's contamination.

He has reunited man to God. That's the main message and goal of this new testament: anyone who believes in Jesus is given the power, through faith, to become a child of God and enjoy a father/child relationship with God even <u>now</u> in this life.

Grace Replaces the Old Law

The old law could not change the sin nature of man nor render man righteous. The law had to be replaced, and this is the reason Jesus had to die as a "sacrifice" to pay for man's sin, and to bring God's <u>grace</u> and mercy to all men.

Ro 10:4 For Christ is the end of the law for righteousness to everyone who believes.

Gal 2:16 Knowing that a man is not justified by the works of the law but by faith in Jesus Christ, even we have believed in Christ Jesus, that we might be justified by faith in Christ and not by the works of the law; for by the works of the law no flesh shall be justified.

Ro 6:14 For sin shall not have dominion over you, for you are not under law but under grace.

2Cor 5:21 For He made Him who knew no sin to be sin for us, that we might become the righteousness of God in Him.

* **Eph 2:8, 9** For by grace you have been saved through faith, and that not of yourselves; it is the gift of God, not of works, lest anyone should boast.

* **Tit 3:5** Not by works of righteousness which we have done, but according to His mercy He saved us, through the washing of regeneration and renewing of the Holy Spirit.

  Ro 5:17 For if by the one man's offense death reigned through the one, much more those who receive abundance of grace and of the gift of righteousness will reign in life through the One, Jesus Christ.

  Ro 11:6 And if by grace, then it is no longer of works; otherwise grace is no longer grace. But if it is of works, it is no longer grace; otherwise work is no longer work.

* **Jn 3:16** For God so loved the world that He gave His only begotten Son, that whoever believes in Him should not perish but have everlasting life.

  Heb 8:12 For I will be merciful to their unrighteousness, and their sins and their lawless deeds I will remember no more.

  Ro 3:20, 23 Therefore by the deeds of the law no flesh will be justified in His sight, for by the law is the knowledge of sin. For all have sinned and fall short of the glory of God, being justified freely by His grace through the redemption that is in Christ Jesus.

* **Ro 6:23** For the wages of sin is death, but the gift of God is eternal life in Christ Jesus our Lord.

  Ro 3:28 Therefore we conclude that a man is justified by faith apart from the deeds of the law.

  Ro 5:6, 8 For when we were still without strength in due time Christ died for the ungodly. But God demonstrates His own love toward us, in that while we were still sinners, Christ died for us.

* **Ro 8:2** For the law of the Spirit of life in Christ Jesus has made me free from the law of sin and death.

* **1Jn 1:9** If we confess our sins, He is faithful and just to forgive us our sins and to cleanse us from all unrighteousness.

Gal 5:4 You have become estranged from Christ, you who attempt to be justified by law; you have fallen from grace.

Heb 4:15, 16 For we do not have a High Priest who cannot sympathize with our weaknesses, but was in all points tempted as we are, yet without sin. Let us therefore come boldly to the throne of grace, that we may obtain mercy and find grace to help in time of need.

* **Jn 1:17** For the law was given through Moses, but grace and truth came through Jesus Christ.

* **Gal 3:13a** Christ has redeemed us from the curse of the law

Eternally Saved through ONE Sacrifice: Jesus

In the old testament, God made a covenant with His people that there had to be a <u>sacrifice</u> of a "lamb without blemish" to forgive man's sins. So, in the new covenant, God Himself offered a "sacrifice" (His lamb without blemish) to redeem mankind of his sin nature so that man could be reunited with God eternally. Christianity is the only religion where a god <u>paid</u> for the redemption of his people. In every other religion man has to attain his holiness through a series of good deeds. But Jesus paid the highest price so that we may be made holy and righteous before God. That is why man's salvation comes through <u>no</u> <u>other</u> than Jesus. For He <u>only</u> has paid the price. So through faith in Jesus and His sacrifice for us, we are given the right to be born into the eternal kingdom of God and can live and <u>operate</u> in it <u>now</u>; not just once we get to Heaven.

Jn 11:25, 26 I am the resurrection and the life. He who believes in Me, though he may die, he shall live. And whoever lives and believes in Me shall never die.

* **Act 4:12** Nor is there salvation in any other, for there is no other name under heaven given among men by which we must be saved.

* **Jn 3:16** For God so loved the world that He gave His only begotten Son, that whoever believes in Him should not perish but have everlasting life.

* **Jn 3:36** He who believes in the Son has everlasting life, and he who does not believe the Son shall not see life, but the wrath of God abides on him.

   Jn 17:3 And this is eternal life, that they may know You, the only true God, and Jesus Christ whom You have sent.

* **Jn 14:6** Jesus said to him, I am the way, the truth, and the life. No one comes to the Father except through Me.

* **Jn 1:12** But as many as received Him, to them He gave the right to become children of God, to those who believe in His name.

* **Mt 18:3** Assuredly, I say to you, unless you are converted and become as little children, you will by no means enter the kingdom of heaven.

* **Jn 3:3b** Unless one is born again, he cannot see the kingdom of God.

* **Act 16:31** Believe on the Lord Jesus Christ, and you will be saved.

   1Tim 2:5 For there is one God and one mediator between God and men, the man Christ Jesus.

* **Jn 6:37** All that the Father gives Me will come to Me, and the one who comes to Me I will by no means cast out.

* **Jn 10:27, 28** My sheep hear My voice, and I know them, and they follow Me. And I give them eternal life, and they shall never perish; neither shall anyone snatch them out of My hand.

* **Ro 3:23** For all have sinned and fall short of the glory of God,

Being Born Again

When we put our faith in Jesus and in the sacrifice of His life for the redemption of mankind, God's Word says that we become <u>born</u> <u>again</u> as a child of God! We become a "new creature" and our spirit is born into the kingdom of God's light!

I. WHAT IS THE NEW TESTAMENT

We are no longer a slave of the world's kingdom of darkness. We take on a <u>new</u> <u>identity</u> as if we'd been given a new passport as a citizen of heaven with every right, privilege and authority of the inheritance that we receive through Jesus, having become <u>co-heirs</u> with Christ.

However, while our spirit is made anew and we've joined in God's kingdom to live in full relationship with God now, our <u>soul</u> (our mind and emotions) along with our <u>physical</u> <u>body</u> are <u>not</u> <u>yet</u> redeemed. But through reading and absorbing the Word of God and letting it change our soul in accordance to the guidelines and principles of His Word, we can renew and discipline our mind and our emotions so that we fully live and operate according to the laws of the kingdom now.

We don't have to wait for heaven to have the full benefits of our new nature, but through faith in what His Word says about us, we can operate in the full inheritance and authority that Jesus gave to all who believe.

* **2Cor 5:17** Therefore, if anyone is in Christ, he is a new creation; old things have passed away; behold, all things have become new.

Col 3:10 Put on the new man who is renewed in knowledge according to the image of Him who created him.

Eph 4:22-24 That you put off, concerning your former conduct, the old man which grows corrupt according to the deceitful lusts, and be renewed in the spirit of your mind, and that you put on the new man which was created according to God, in true righteousness and holiness.

Gal 2:20 I have been crucified with Christ; it is no longer I who live, but Christ lives in me; and the life which I now live in the flesh I live by faith in the Son of God, who loved me and gave Himself for me.

* **Ro 10:9, 10** If you confess with your mouth the Lord Jesus and believe in your heart that God has raised Him from the dead, you will be saved. For with the heart one believes unto righteousness, and with the mouth confession is made unto salvation.

Ro 8:17 And if children, then heirs—heirs of God and joint heirs with Christ, if indeed we suffer with Him, that we may also be glorified together.

1Pt 1:23 Having been born again, not of corruptible seed but incorruptible, through the word of God which lives and abides forever.

Ro 6:4 Therefore we were buried with Him through baptism into death, that just as Christ was raised from the dead by the glory of the Father, even so we also should walk in newness of life.

Phil 3:13,14 Brethren, I do not count myself to have apprehended; but one thing I do, forgetting those things which are behind and reaching forward to those things which are ahead, I press toward the goal for the prize of the upward call of God in Christ Jesus.

* **1Pt 2:2** As newborn babes, desire the pure milk of the word, that you may grow thereby.

1Cor 6:19, 20 Do you not know that your body is the temple of the Holy Spirit who is in you, whom you have from God, and you are not your own? For you were bought at a price; therefore glorify God in your body and in your spirit, which are God's.

1Pt 1:3 Blessed be the God and Father of our Lord Jesus Christ, who according to His great mercy has caused us to be born again to a living hope through the resurrection of Jesus Christ from the dead

Our New Identity in Christ

We cannot truly become like Jesus and be empowered to enforce the kingdom of God on earth unless we embrace the new identity that we have in Christ. We have been created anew, and are empowered against the devices of the enemy and we also have authority to destroy the enemy's works here on earth. That changes everything.

Being born again is only the first part of our new creation. Our mind has to be fully renewed to the truth of what Jesus says about us, and who He is in us. If that doesn't take place, our mind and body will not be operating in the new identity of Christ in us. We're no longer our own. It's Jesus in us that conquers evil around us.

It's only when we allow the Word to fully renew our mind so that our body is in subjection and in obedience to the Word, that Jesus can empower us so that we can be full-on ambassadors of the kingdom of God here on Earth. Then and only then our new identity can be noticed by others because we're letting the Lord continue to be here amongst men, bringing His kingdom on earth and destroying the works of the devil. (See "Boldness of Righteousness")

Col 3:1-3 If then you were <u>raised</u> with Christ, seek those things which are above, where Christ is, sitting at the right hand of God. Set your mind on things above, not on things on the earth. For you <u>died</u>, and your life is hidden with Christ in God.

1Pt 2:9 But you are a chosen generation, a royal priesthood, a holy nation, His own special people, that you may proclaim the praises of Him who called you out of darkness into His marvelous light.

Gen 1:27 So God created man in His own image; in the image of God He created him; male and female He created them.

1Jn 3:1, 2a Behold what manner of love the Father has bestowed on us, that we should be called children of God! Therefore the world does not know us, because it did not know Him. Beloved, now we are children of God.

Gal 3:27, 28 For as many of you as were baptized into Christ have put on Christ. There is neither Jew nor Greek, there is neither slave nor free, there is neither male nor female; for you are all one in Christ Jesus.

Col 2:9, 10 For in Him dwells all the fullness of the Godhead bodily; and you are <u>complete in Him</u>, who is the head of all principality and power.

Eph 1:5 Having predestined us to <u>adoption as sons</u> by Jesus Christ to Himself, according to the good pleasure of His will.

1Cor 6:17 But he who is joined to the Lord is one spirit with Him.

Ro 6:6 Knowing this, that our old man was crucified with Him, that the body of sin might be done away with, that we should no longer be slaves of sin.

1Cor 12:27 Now you are the body of Christ, and members individually.

1Cor 6:19, 20 Or do you not know that your body is the temple of the Holy Spirit who is in you, whom you have from God, and you are not your own? For you were bought at a price; therefore glorify God in your body and in your spirit, which are God's.

Eph 2:5 Even when we were dead in trespasses, made us alive together with Christ (by grace you have been saved).

The Power of Declarations

If we want to operate in the spirit of the new creation that we have been made into, so as to fully believe what God says about us, renewing our mind is <u>imperative</u>. So, to say aloud what the Word of God says about us is a key to conforming our thought pattern to the truth. The following declarations, also called confessions, are based on what the Word of God says about our newborn identity. Since our old man has died, we can now live in the faith and in the authority of the new man we have become through Christ.

Read aloud and meditate on these often to declare and proclaim your new identity, personality and behavior as a child of the kingdom of God. These declarations will change the belief system in your heart in order for your mind to operate in accordance to who you've become. (You may want to look up the references in your Bible, to further understand those statements of faith.)

Ro 5:10 I am reconciled to God through Christ's death and saved through Christ's life.

1Pt 1:18, 19 I am redeemed by the blood of Jesus.

* **Gal 3:13** I am redeemed from the curse of the law.

I. WHAT IS THE NEW TESTAMENT

Ro 8:17 I am a child of God and a co-heir with Christ.

Ro 6:6 I am no longer a slave to sin.

Eph 1:1 I am a saint.

Ro 6:18 I am set free from sin and a slave of righteousness.

Acts 13:39 I am forgiven through Christ.

2Cor 5:17 I am a new creation.

2Cor 5:21 I am righteous in Christ.

Jn 14:20 I am indwelled by Christ. His Spirit lives in me.

Ro 8:2 I am free in Christ.

Ro 8:1 I am free from condemnation.

Jn 15:15, 16 I am a branch of the True Vine and I am chosen and appointed by Christ to go and bear fruit.

Mt 5:13 I am the salt of the earth.

Mt 5:14 I am the light of the world.

Mt 6:26 I am valuable to God.

Ro 8:37 I am more than a conqueror through Christ.

Ro 15:7 I am accepted by Christ.

* **1Cor 2:16** I have the mind of Christ.

1Cor 3:16 I am a temple of God. His Spirit lives in me.

1Cor 6:11 I am washed, justified, and sanctified through Christ.

2Cor 12:27 I am part of Christ's body.

2Cor 2:15 I am the fragrance of Christ.

2Cor 5:20 I am an ambassador for Christ of reconciliation.

Eph 1:3 I am blessed with every spiritual blessings.

1Jn 2:27 I am anointed with the Holy Spirit.

Jn 15:9 I am loved.

Jn 17:17 I am sanctified by the truth.

Jn 17:15 I am protected from the evil one.

1Pt 1:16 I am holy through Christ.

Isa 61:1 I am free from darkness.

Ro 1:7 I am beloved of God.

Ro 5:1 I am justified by faith.

Heb 13:5 I am not forsaken.

Ro 6:11 I am alive in Christ.

1Thes 1:10 I am rescued by Jesus.

The Boldness of Righteousness

The word "righteous" comes up 558 times in the Bible, so righteousness is important to God. Jesus' sacrifice on the cross has made us righteous before God. *"For He made Him who knew no sin to be sin for us, that we might become the righteousness of God in Him" (2 Cor 5:21)*.

Because God is righteous, He wants us to not only be righteous but live righteously. *"Because God is holy He wants us to be holy as He is holy"(1Pet 1:15)*. Grace has made us holy and righteous in spirit; but to walk out that righteousness, we must be renewed in the spirit of our mind by the Word and obey it. Grace without obedience is not truly grace. God's grace does not free us to sin, it frees us from sin.

Obedience is very important to God. Samuel, the prophet, rebuked King Saul by saying, *"To obey is better than sacrifice" (1Sam 15:22)*, because the spirit of rebellion is the very essence of sin. Disobedience is the repudiation of God's authority. On the other hand, king David said, *"I delight to do Your will, O my God" (Ps 40:8)*. God requires our obedience because it shows that we love and trust Him.

Jesus said, *"He who has My commandments and keeps them, it is he who loves Me" (Jn 14:21)* and *"If you keep My commandments, you will abide in My love," (Jn 15:10)* and *"Blessed are those who do His commandments, that they may have the right to the tree of life" (Rev 22:14)*. Even Jesus walked in full submission and obedience to the Father. He said, *"I always do those things that please Him" (Jn 8:29)*.

You can become fearless, confident, and relentless in the pursuit of what you seek when you have the conviction that what you are doing is what you are supposed to be doing.

The righteous are also referred to as "blameless". It is a purity of heart that comes from trust and obedience. It carries the truth, the power of God's Word through an obedient life. Righteousness brings on great rewards. One of those rewards is boldness. *"The righteous are bold as a lion" (Pro 28:1)*.

Obedience is walking in righteousness and it gives you boldness and confidence to walk up to the throne of grace and obtain mercy. Grace takes out of us all reluctance to obey. Through the atonement of Jesus, man is able to obey because that atonement enables sufficient grace; rebellion is removed, and gladness and joy are supplied along with love and trust. The apostle Paul said, *"The love of Christ compels me" (2 Cor 5:14)*.

Think of a healthy parental relationship where the child is obedient. He can walk in total freedom, confidence and boldness in the father's love. *"If you keep My commandments, you will abide in My love" (Jn 15:10)*. *"We receive from Him, because we keep His commandments and do those things that are pleasing in His sight" (1Jn 3:22)*.

God's commands are not grievous, meaning that they're not hard to keep, because they are founded in right-ness, in justice and in wisdom. The Word of God teaches us what to do; but James 4:17 says that sinning is knowing what to do and <u>not doing</u> it. If we desire free access to God in prayer, then each obstacle of disobedience and sin should be removed. Otherwise condemnation sets in and renders our approach to Him weak.

An obedient life is not simply a reformed life. It is not the old life primed and painted with good resolutions, but rather a life where the will is in full conformity to God's will and the heart is in full intimacy with God's heart. Obedient men are always closest to God.

Religious faith, which tolerates sinning, has no power in prayer and no boldness in performance. *"Why do you call Me 'Lord, Lord,' and do not do the things which I say" (Lk 6:46)*. Those who are wholly separated unto God bring energy, force and flame in praying and in their conduct. *"For the eyes of the Lord run to and fro throughout the whole earth, to show Himself strong on behalf of those whose heart is loyal to Him" (2Chr 16:9)*. It is the doing that gives potency to the Christian life (Mt 7:24-27).

Does this mean that we will not sin any more if we are Christians? No, it does not. In Paul's letter to the believers at Corinth, we find some things that seem hard to understand. On the one hand, Paul calls these believers "saints"— "holy ones," and he says that they are *"sanctified [set apart] in Christ Jesus" (1Cor 1:2)*. On the other hand, in the same letter, Paul speaks of some terrible sins in their lives. Some were proud, some fought among themselves, and some were guilty of downright immoral acts. What is the explanation of this? How could Paul say that they were "saints" while at the same time they were not living as Christians should live? To answer these questions, we must understand the difference between our position and our walk. The believer's standing in Christ is perfect and unchanging. Our spirit is redeemed and we're in right-standing with God. But there is the matter of our daily walk to reflect this cleansing. And this is done through following Christ closely in obedience.

Conduct is the outward life, whereas character is the life unseen yet evidenced by an intimate relationship with God. You may say character is the roots of the tree whereas our conduct is the leaves. Any alleged form of a Christian which does not reflect a holy character is a delusion and a snare *(Jn 1:22)*. Obedience produces cleanliness of heart and purity of life and boldness of character. God looks on the heart and the motives of the heart.

Ro 6:1, 2 What shall we say then? Shall we continue in sin that grace may abound? Certainly not! How shall we who died to sin live any longer in it?

Ro 6:4 Therefore we were buried with Him through baptism into death, that just as Christ was raised from the dead by the glory of the Father, even so we also should walk in newness of life.

Ro 6:10-12 For the death that He died, He died to sin once for all; but the life that He lives, He lives to God. Likewise you also, reckon yourselves to be dead indeed to sin, but alive to God in Christ Jesus our Lord. Therefore do not let sin reign in your mortal body, that you should obey it in its lusts.

Ro 6:13 And do not present your members as instruments of unrighteousness to sin, but present yourselves to God as being alive from the dead, and your members as instruments of righteousness to God.

Ro 6:18 And having been set free from sin, you became slaves of righteousness.

1Jn 3:10 In this the children of God and the children of the devil are manifest: whoever does not practice righteousness is not of God, nor is he who does not love his brother.

Act 10:34-35 Then Peter opened his mouth and said: "In truth I perceive that God shows no partiality. But in every nation whoever fears Him and works righteousness is accepted by Him.

Tit 2:11, 12 For the grace of God that brings salvation has appeared to all men, teaching us that, denying ungodliness and worldly lusts, we should live soberly, righteously, and godly in the present age.

Pr 4:18 But the path of the just is like the shining sun, that shines ever brighter unto the perfect day.

Ro 6:16 Do you not know that to whom you present yourselves slaves to obey, you are that one's slaves whom you obey, whether of sin leading to death, or of obedience leading to righteousness?

Pr 10:6-7, 11, 25 Blessings are on the head of the righteous, but violence covers the mouth of the wicked. The memory of the righteous is blessed, But the name of the wicked will rot. The mouth of the righteous is a well of life, but violence covers the mouth of the wicked. When the whirlwind passes by, the wicked is no more, but the righteous has an everlasting foundation.

Mt 13:43 Then the righteous will shine forth as the sun in the kingdom of their Father. He who has ears to hear, let him hear!

Isa 32:17 The work of righteousness will be peace, And the effect of righteousness, quietness and assurance forever.

2Tim 4:7, 8 I have fought the good fight, I have finished the race, I have kept the faith. Finally, there is laid up for me the crown of righteousness, which the Lord, the righteous Judge, will give to me on that day, and not to me only but also to all who have loved His appearing.

2Cor 7:1 Therefore, having these promises, beloved, let us cleanse ourselves from all filthiness of the flesh and spirit, perfecting holiness in the fear of God.

Ro 6:22 But now having been set free from sin, and having become slaves of God, you have your fruit to holiness, and the end, everlasting life.

Mt 5:48 Therefore you shall be perfect, just as your Father in heaven is perfect.

II. GOD'S GIFT TO NEW BELIEVERS: THE HOLY SPIRIT

Jesus promised to send the Holy Spirit to live in us. He said that He will not leave us comfortless, but that He will send us the Spirit of the Father which will lead us into all truth, and give us power to live our Christian lives (Acts 1:8).

Some people say, "Well, how do you expect me to be like Jesus or live as exemplary a life as He did?" This is the very reason why the Holy Spirit of God was provided to us as well. This is the same Holy Spirit which Jesus received when baptized by John the Baptist which empowered Him to operate in the Spirit here on Earth, even though a man (Mt 3:16-17).

Jesus had His disciples wait in Jerusalem so that when the infilling of the Holy Spirit came, they would have the power to win many others to Him. That was the main purpose of the Day of Pentecost; not just the supernatural manifestations that took place. The outpouring of the Holy Spirit on the disciples was to empower them.

The Holy Spirit empowers us with the Words of God, giving us faith to stand up for the truth and boldly share our faith with others. Jesus said that all believers can receive the baptism of the Holy Spirit by simply asking the Father to give Him to us (Lk 11:13).

The Spirit of Truth and the Power of God

* **Lk 11:13** If you then, being evil, know how to give good gifts to your children, how much more will your heavenly Father give the Holy Spirit to those who ask Him.

* **Acts 1:8** You shall receive power when the Holy Spirit has come upon you; and you shall be witnesses to Me in Jerusalem, and in all Judea and Samaria, and to the ends of the earth.

* **Jn 14:26** But the helper, the Holy Spirit, whom the Father will send in My name, He will teach you all things, and bring to your remembrance all things that I said to you.

Eph 3:16 That He would grant you, according to the riches of His glory, to be strengthened with might through His Spirit in the inner man.

Lk 3:16 John answered, saying to all, "I indeed baptize you with water; but One mightier than I is coming, whose sandal strap I am not worthy to loose. He will baptize you with the Holy Spirit and fire.

Acts 2:38 Then Peter said to them, "Repent, and let every one of you be baptized in the name of Jesus Christ for the remission of sins; and you shall receive the gift of the Holy Spirit."

* **Acts 4:31** And when they had prayed, the place where they were assembled together was shaken; and they were all filled with the Holy Spirit, and they spoke the Word of God with boldness.

Acts 2:3, 4 Then there appeared to them divided tongues, as of fire, and one sat upon each of them. And they were all filled with the Holy Spirit and began to speak with other tongues, as the Spirit gave them utterance.

Gal 5:18 But if you are led by the Spirit, you are not under the law.

* **Gal 5:22** The fruit of the Spirit is love, joy, peace, longsuffering, kindness, goodness, faithfulness, gentleness, self-control. Against such there is no law.

Lk 4:18, 19 The Spirit of the Lord is upon Me, Because He has anointed Me to preach the gospel to the poor; He has sent Me to heal the brokenhearted, to proclaim liberty to the captives and recovery of sight to the blind. To set at liberty those who are oppressed; To proclaim the acceptable year of the Lord.

Jn 7:38, 39 He who believes in Me, as the scripture has said, out of his heart will flow rivers of living water. But this He spoke concerning the Spirit, whom those believing in Him would receive; for the Holy Spirit was not yet given, because Jesus was not yet glorified.

II. GOD'S GIFT TO NEW BELIEVERS: THE HOLY SPIRIT

Ro 14:17 For the kingdom of God is not what is eaten and not what is being drunk, but righteousness and peace and joy in the Holy Spirit.

1Cor 12:8-11 For to one is given the word of wisdom through the Spirit, to another the word of knowledge through the same Spirit, to another faith by the same Spirit, to another gifts of healings by the same Spirit, to another the working of miracles, to another prophecy, to another discerning of spirits, to another different kinds of tongues, to another the interpretation of tongues. But one and the same Spirit works all these things, distributing to each one individually as He wills.

2Cor 3:17 Now the Lord is the Spirit; and where the Spirit of the Lord is, there is liberty.

Eph 5:18b, 19 But be filled with the Spirit, speaking to one another in psalms and hymns and spiritual songs, singing and making melody in your heart to the Lord.

Jude 1:20 But you, beloved, building yourselves up on your most holy faith, praying in the Holy Spirit.

* **Acts 2:17, 18** And it shall come to pass in the last days, says God, that I will pour out of My Spirit on all flesh; Your sons and your daughters shall prophesy, your young men shall see visions, your old men shall dream dreams. And on My menservants and on My maidservants I will pour out My Spirit in those days.

* **Jn 16:13** However, when He, the Spirit of truth, has come, He will guide you into all truth; for He will not speak on His own authority, but whatever He hears He will speak; and He will tell you things to come.

The Gift of Tongues

The kingdom of God exceeds the knowledge that our finite mind can grasp, but the gift of tongues allows our spirit to connect with the Spirit of God and reveal to us truth, knowledge, understanding and wisdom. It is a great exercise of our faith to speak in tongues because it bypasses our mind and taps into our spirit, which we cannot see nor feel. Tongues is fanning the fire of God in us, like a dynamo to our faith. Jesus said that the gift of tongues is part of the signs that follow them that believe (Mk 16:17).

The gift of tongues is particularly useful when we pray because when we don't know what to pray for, praying in tongues will allow the Holy Spirit in us to make intercession on our behalf.

* **Ro 8:26, 27** Likewise the Spirit also helps in our weaknesses. For we do not know what we should pray for as we ought, but the Spirit Himself makes intercession for us with groaning which cannot be uttered. Now He who searches the hearts knows what the mind of the Spirit is, because He makes intercession for the saints according to the <u>will of God</u>.

Acts 2:1-4 When the day of Pentecost had fully come, they were all with one accord in one place. And suddenly there came a sound from heaven, as of a rushing mighty wind, and it filled the whole house where they were sitting. Then there appeared to them divided tongues, as of fire, and one sat upon each one of them. And they were all filled with the Holy Spirit and began to speak with other tongues, as the Spirit gave them utterance.

1Cor 14:2 For he who speaks in a tongue does not speak to men but to God, for no one understands him; however, in the Spirit he speaks mysteries.

Acts 19:6, 7 When Paul had laid hands on them, the Holy Spirit came upon them, and they spoke with tongues and prophesied.

1Cor 14:39 Therefore, brethren, desire earnestly to prophesy, and do not forbid to speak with tongues.

Acts 10:44-46 While Peter was still speaking these words, the Holy Spirit fell upon all those who heard the word. And those of the circumcision who believed were astonished, as many as came with Peter, because the gift of the Holy Spirit had been poured out on the Gentiles also. For they heard them speak with tongues and magnify God.

II. GOD'S GIFT TO NEW BELIEVERS: THE HOLY SPIRIT

Hearing from God

Do you want to know how to hear God's voice? --To know how He speaks to you? One of the first and best ways to hear His voice is to become familiar with His Word. As more time is spent meditating upon the Word of God, the more sensitive we will become to that "still small voice" speaking to our heart.

The Holy Spirit opens up our understanding when reading God's Word. He makes the Word come <u>alive</u> to us so that we can hear God's voice, that inner witness. Jesus said, *"My sheep hear My voice" (Jn 10:27)*. He often quickens a passage or verse to us, applying it to our own personal situation, and He brings the Word to life just for us! All of a sudden it hits our heart and we really get His point! *"The entrance of Thy Word giveth light, it giveth understanding to the simple" (Psa.119:130)*.

Jn 8:47a He who is of God hears God's words.

Jn 6:63 It is the Spirit who gives life; the flesh profits nothing. The words that I speak to you are Spirit, and they are life.

Lk 12:12 For the Holy Spirit will teach you in that very hour what you ought to say.

Ps 119:105 Your word is a lamp to my feet and a light to my path.

Heb 8:10 For this is the covenant that I will make with the house of Israel after those days, says the Lord: I will put My laws in their mind and write them on their hearts; and I will be their God, and they shall be My people.

2Tim 3:16, 17 All scripture is given by inspiration of God, and is profitable for doctrine, for reproof, for correction, for instruction in righteousness, that the man of God may be complete, thoroughly equipped for every good work.

* **Heb 4:12** For the Word of God is living and powerful, and sharper than any two-edged sword, piercing even to the division of soul and spirit, and of joints and marrow, and is a discerner of the thoughts and intents of the heart.

Jn 5:30 I can of Myself do nothing. As I hear, I judge; and My judgment is righteous, because I do not seek My own will but the will of the Father who sent Me.

Ro 8:16 The Spirit Himself bears witness with our spirit that we are children of God.

* **Pr 3:5, 6** Trust in the Lord with all your heart, and lean not on your own understanding; In all your ways acknowledge Him, and He shall direct your paths.

* **Isa 30:21** Your ears shall hear a word behind you, saying, "This is the way, walk in it," Whenever you turn to the right hand or whenever you turn to the left.

Jn 10:27 My sheep hear My voice, and I know them, and they follow Me.

Col 3:15 And let the peace of God rule in your hearts.

* **Amos 3:7** Surely the Lord God does nothing, Unless He reveals His secret to His servants the prophets.

* **Ps 32:8** I will instruct you and teach you in the way you should go; I will guide you with My eye.

* **Pr 1:23b** I will pour out my spirit on you; I will make my words known to you.

* **Isa 42:9** Behold, the former things have come to pass, And new things I declare; Before they spring forth I tell you of them.

* **Jer 23:28** The prophet who has a dream, let him tell a dream; And he who has My word, let him speak My word faithfully.

* **Ps 73:24a** You will guide me with Your counsel.

* **Jer 1:9b** I Have put My words in your mouth

III. THE LIVING WORD OF GOD

God's Word is <u>His</u> standard, and a solid <u>rock</u> to build on. He honors His Word above His name! In the parable of the sower, Jesus said, *"The kingdom of God is like a farmer who sows seeds" (Mk 4:26)*, and later He said that the <u>seed</u> is the <u>Word</u> of God, and once <u>buried</u> in our hearts, will bring forth its fruit.

Reading, absorbing and following the Word of God is the most important thing we can do because it's the Word that keeps us in tune with God. In fact, this entire era and age of grace is built on us having faith in the Word! *"For without faith, it is impossible to please God" (Heb.11:6)*. God expects us, His children, to "walk by faith" in His Word. And since faith comes from His Word, we must eagerly absorb His Word for ourselves, and thereby gain the faith that we need to meet the needs and confront the situations we face. This is why the Word is so important! It is the primary means by which we receive God's communication and are made aware of His will.

His Word is the known, sure, absolute, revealed will of God! Jesus said, *"The words that I speak unto you, they are spirit and they are life" (John 6:63)*. His Word is what gives us spiritual life and food and nourishment and strength and health! This is why a good wholesome balanced diet of His Word is essential if you wish to grow and stay close to Him.

Jesus Himself is called *"The Word of God"*. *(Rev.19:13; Jn.1:1, 14)*. Just like you have to eat in order to have physical strength, you have to feed from the Word, drink of the Word, to have spiritual strength. The Prophet Jeremiah said, *"I found Thy Words and did eat them, and Thy Word was unto me the joy and rejoicing of my heart" (Jer.15:16)*. And Job said, *"I have esteemed the Words of His mouth more than my necessary food" (Job 23:12)*. There's nothing more important to your spiritual life than the Word.

Jesus said, *"But one thing is needed, and Mary has chosen that good part, which will not be taken away from her" (Luk.10:42)*. If you put the Word first, the Lord will always give you time somehow to take care of the other things. The minute you start crowding the Word out of your life, you are getting too busy! Try to set aside time each day in which you can quietly <u>commune</u> with the Lord through His Word. When you see the difference it makes in your walk with the Lord, you'll wonder how you ever got by without it! We are what we read and what we're hungry for.

It is important to read the Word in a prayerful and receptive attitude, looking to His Holy Spirit for guidance to open up the eyes of our hearts. It says, *"The natural man receiveth not the things of the Spirit of God, for they are foolishness unto him, neither can he know them, because they are spiritually discerned" (1Cor.2:14)*. So we must ask the Holy Spirit for the discernment needed to understand His Word. The Holy Spirit is the One who'll reveal things to us and lead us into all truth. That's why we must pray and ask Him to: *"Give unto us the spirit of wisdom and revelation so the eyes of our understanding will be enlightened" (Eph 1:17,18)*. David prayed, *"Open thou mine eyes that I may behold wondrous things out of Thy law" (Psa.119:18)*. The more the Holy Spirit reveals the Word to you, the more you will find that God will speak to you loudly and clearly and directly through His written Word!

A lot has to do with your own desire to hear from the Lord and your own personal hunger and receptivity. *"Blessed are those who hunger and thirst for righteousness, for they shall be filled" (Mat.5:6; Luk.1:53)*.

So much has to do with our attitude. The Scribes and the Pharisees of Jesus' day were fluent in scripture, they knew it by heart, and they copied it all the time by hand. But because they were so self-satisfied and self-righteous, they were anything but *"hungering and thirsting after righteousness"*, and their hearts were hardened and their spiritual ears were deaf and they were devoid of understanding! They resisted the truth of the Word that they read, and truth resisted loses its power over the mind. They didn't even realise how spiritually alienated they were from the Lord.

So read the Word prayerfully and thoughtfully. You can miss a lot of the meaning, the real depth of what the Lord's talking about, unless you stop to really think about it and apply the Word to your personal situation; that's what meditating on the Word is all about. If you will diligently and prayerfully labour in His Word, He will greatly reward you. *"The law of your mouth is better to me than thousands of coins of gold and silver" (Psa.119:72).*

If you want to get a taste of the many benefits of reading the Word, read Psalm 1. *"But his delight is in the law of the Lord, and in his law he meditates day and night. He shall be like a tree, planted by the rivers of water that brings forth his fruit in his season, whose leaf also shall not wither; and whatever he does shall prosper" (Psa.1:2, 3).*

Regardless of how backslidden and dried up you are, the water of His Word can bring you to life again; into a virtual resurrection if you will soak in His Word! The more you study the Word and really dig into the Word, the more it will become refreshing and a continuous source of guidance to you. Soaking in the Word will rekindle in your heart a desire to change, because you will be inspired, envisioned, revitalized, renewed, invigorated, challenged, enthused and filled with faith from His Words!

The secret of power and victory and overcoming and fruitfulness and fire and life and warmth and light and leadership is the Word! And the lack of the Word is the secret of backsliding and failure and coldness and darkness and weakness and dying spiritually! Jesus said, *"As the branch cannot bear fruit of itself except it abide in the vine, no more can ye except ye abide in Me" (Jn.15:4,7).* Even your ministry to others is not as important as getting into the Word yourself first! You'll never have the spiritual strength and stamina or the spirit needed, unless you yourself are drinking in the Word and being spiritually nourished and strengthened by it yourself first.

If you're weak in faith, it's because you're weak in the Word. If you're having battles with doubts, the best cure is the Word! The best way to build up your faith is to bury yourself in the Word of God! Let His truth cleanse you and rid you of all the filth of this rotten old world and your own sinful heart! *"You are already clean because of the word which I have spoken to you" (Jn.15:3. Rom: 12:2). "How can a young man cleanse his way? By taking heed according to your word"(Psa.119:9; Eph.5:26).*

The Word is what really draws the line that separates you from the world and from the worldlings. *"He who is of God hears God's words; therefore you do not hear, because you are not of God" (Jn.8:47; 1Jn.4:5, 6). "The law of his God is in his heart, none of his steps shall slide" (Psa.37:31).*

The Word is also our weapon! *"The sword of the spirit, which is the word of God" (Eph.6:17).* It is our spiritual sword that drives away and defeats the devil every time we use it! When Jesus Himself was tempted by the devil, He fought back with the Word *(See Mat.4:1-10)*. So when the Enemy comes around, take out your sword and whack away! He can't stand the Word! The best way to put the Enemy out of action is with the Word! Just bury him in a flood of truth! And he and all of his doubts and fears will flee!

The Word is also a light that drives away and defeats the Enemy's darkness! *"Thy Word is a Lamp unto my feet and a light unto my path" (Psa.119:105).* When you fill your mind with the Word of God, you don't have room for the darkness. When the devil attacks you with his doubts and his fears and his discouragement and his temptations and all the rest, turn on the light of God's Word and the shadows will flee! Read it, quote it, sing it, and claim it! It never fails!

And also, when ministering to others, use the Word. There is absolute power in the Words of God. It is only the sword of His Spirit which is sharp enough to pierce the hardest armour, so that the warmth of His Spirit of love can flow into their empty hearts.

The more you live in the Word, the closer you'll be to the Lord, and the more blessed and fruitful your life will be!

Jesus is the Word of God ~ The Creator

God created the universe by His spoken Word. In the Book of John, the first chapter, there is an explanation of Jesus being the Word of God.

III. THE LIVING WORD OF GOD

Heb 11:3 By faith we understand that the worlds were framed by the Word of God, so that the things which are seen were not made of things which are visible.

Jn 1:1-3 In the beginning was the Word, and the word was with God, and the Word was God. He was in the beginning with God. All things were made through Him, and without Him nothing was made that was made.

Jn 1:14 And the Word became flesh and dwelt among us, and we beheld His glory, the glory as of the only begotten of the Father, full of grace and truth.

Heb 1:10 You, Lord, in the beginning laid the foundation of the earth, and the heavens are the work of Your hands.

Ps 33:6, 9 By the Word of the Lord the heavens were made, for He spoke, and it was done; He commanded, and it stood fast.

Ps 138:2b For You have magnified Your Word above all Your name.

Heb 1:3 Who being the brightness of His glory and the express image of His person, and upholding all things by the Word of His power, when He had by Himself purged our sins, sat down at the right hand of the Majesty on high.

Rev 19:11-13 Now I saw heaven opened, and behold, a white horse. And He who sat on him was called Faithful and True, and in righteousness He judges and makes war. His eyes were like a flame of fire, and on His head were many crowns. He had a name written that no one knew except Himself. He was clothed with a robe dipped in blood, and His name is called the Word of God.

God's Word cannot Fail

God has invested His power in His Word. It is an incorruptible seed and He cannot fail His Word.

1Kg 8:56b There has not failed one word of all His good promise, which He promised through His servant Moses.

Ps 119:89 Forever, O Lord, Your word is settled in heaven.

Ps 119:160 The entirety of Your word is truth, and every one of Your righteous judgments endures forever..

Isa 40:8 The grass withers, the flower fades, but the word of our God stands forever.

Isa 55:10, 11 For as the rain comes down, and the snow from heaven, and do not return there, but water the earth, and make it bring forth and bud, that it may give seed to the sower and bread to the eater, so shall My word be that goes forth from My mouth; It shall not return to Me void, but it shall accomplish what I please, and it shall prosper in the thing for which I sent it.

* **Jos 23:14b** Not one thing has failed of all the good things which the Lord your God spoke concerning you. All have come to pass for you; not one word of them has failed.

* **Mt 24:35** Heaven and earth will pass away, but My words will by no means pass away.

1Pt 1:25a But the word of the Lord endures forever.

* **Heb 4:12** For the word of God is living and powerful, and sharper than any two-edged sword, piercing even to the division of soul and spirit, and of joints and marrow, and is a discerner of the thoughts and intents of the heart.

The <u>Benefits</u> of knowing God's Word

Jesus said, *"Abide in Me and I in you. As the <u>branch cannot bring fruit</u> of itself unless it abides in the vine, neither can you unless you abide in Me" (Jn 15:4)*. This is the <u>key</u> to a fruitful Christian life–<u>abiding</u> in the Word!

* **Jn 8:31b, 32** If you abide in My word, you are My disciples indeed. And you shall know the truth, and the truth shall make you free.

Jn 15:5 I am the vine, you are the branches. He who abides in Me, and I in him, bears much fruit; for without Me you can do nothing.

III. THE LIVING WORD OF GOD

* **Ps 1:3** He shall be like a tree planted by the rivers of water, that brings forth its fruit in its season, whose leaf also shall not wither; and whatever he does shall prosper.
* **Ps 37:31** The law of his God is in his heart; none of his steps shall slide.

  Ps 19:7 The law of the Lord is perfect, converting the soul; the testimony of the Lord is sure, making wise the simple.

  Ps 119:9 How can a young man cleanse his way? By taking heed according to Your word.

  Ps 119:105 Your word is a lamp to my feet and a light to my path.
* **Ps 119:165** Great peace have those who love Your law, and nothing causes them to stumble.

  Josh 1:8 This book of the law shall not depart from your mouth, but you shall meditate in it day and night, that you may observe to do according to all that is written in it. For then you will make your way prosperous, and then you will have good success.
* **Jn 15:3** You are already clean because of the word which I have spoken to you.
* **Ro 10:17** So then faith comes by hearing, and hearing by the Word of God.
* **2Pt 1:4** By which have been given to us exceedingly great and precious promises, that through these you may be partakers of the divine nature, having escaped the corruption that is in the world through lust.

  Job 23:12 I have not departed from the commandment of His lips; I have treasured the words of His mouth more than my necessary food.

  Ps 119:72 The law of Your mouth is better to me than thousands of gold and silver.

  Jn 15:11 These things I have spoken to you, that My joy may remain in you, and that your joy may be full.

Ps 1:1-3 Blessed is the man who walks not in the counsel of the ungodly, nor stands in the path of sinners, nor sits in the seat of the scornful; But his delight is in the law of the Lord, and in His law he meditates day and night. He shall be like a tree planted by the rivers of water that brings forth its fruit in its season, whose leaf also shall not wither; and whatever he does shall prosper.

* **Ps 119:11** Your word I have hidden in my heart, That I might not sin against You.

Study and Meditate on God's Word

Jesus said, *"Come unto Me all you who are heavy laden and I will give you rest" (Mt. 11:28)*. The way to read God's Word is to let it impregnate you with its truth. It is not enough to just read it, but we must meditate on it to the degree that it saturates our heart. God made the whole world operate from seeds and their reproduction. The Word of God is a "seed book". The ground is your heart, not your head. Get the seeds below the surface by speaking the Word into your heart. As we meditate on the Word, faith rises inside of us.

1Tim 4:15 Meditate on these things; give yourself entirely to them, that your progress may be evident to all.

Pro 4:20-22 My son, give attention to my words; Incline your ear to my sayings. Do not let them depart from your eyes; keep them in the midst of your heart; For they are life to those who find them, and health to all their flesh.

* **Jn 6:63** It is the Spirit who gives life; the flesh profits nothing. The words that I speak to you are spirit, and they are life.

Ps 1:2 But His delight is in the law of the Lord, and in His law he meditates day and night.

Ps 119:97 Oh, how I love Your law! It is my meditation all the day.

Ps 119:99b For Your testimonies are my meditation.

* **Ps 119:130** The entrance of Your words gives light; It gives understanding to the simple.

III. THE LIVING WORD OF GOD

* **Mt 4:4b** Man shall not live by bread alone, but by every word that proceeds from the mouth of God.
* **2Tim 2:15** Be diligent to present yourself approved to God, a worker who does not need to be ashamed, rightly dividing the word of truth.
* **1Pt 2:2** As newborn babes, desire the pure milk of the word, that you may grow thereby.

Obedience is the Key~Faith without Works is Dead

Jesus said that <u>hearing</u> His Word will not transform us, but it is in the <u>doing</u> and walking out His Word that makes it <u>work</u> its power in us (Mt 7:24-27). (See "The Boldness of Righteousness")

Mt 7:24-27 Therefore whoever hears these sayings of Mine, and does them, I will liken him to a wise man who <u>built his house</u> on the <u>rock</u>: and the rain descended, the floods came, and the winds blew and beat on that house; and it <u>did not fall</u>, for it was founded on the rock. But everyone who hears these sayings of Mine, and <u>does not</u> do them, will be like a foolish man who built his house on the sand: and the rain descended, the floods came, and the winds blew and beat on that house; and it fell and great was its fall.

* **Jam 1:22-25** But be doers of the word, and not hearers only, deceiving yourselves. For if anyone is a hearer of the word and not a doer, he is like a man observing his natural face in a mirror; for he observes himself, goes away, and immediately forgets what kind of man he was. But he who looks into the perfect law of liberty and continues in it, and is not a forgetful hearer but a doer of the work, this one will be blessed in what he does.
* **Jn 13:17** If you know these things, blessed are you if you do them.

Isa 1:19 If you are willing and obedient, you shall eat the good of the land.

Ps 119:34 Give me understanding, and I shall keep Your law; indeed, I shall observe it with my whole heart.

* **Jn 14:15** If you love Me, keep My commandments.

  Jn 14:21, 23 He who has My commandments and keeps them, it is he who loves Me and he who loves Me will be loved by My Father, and I will love him and manifest Myself to him. Jesus answered and said to him, "If anyone loves Me, he will <u>keep My word</u>; and My Father will love him, and we will come to him and make our home with him."

* **Jn 15:14** You are My friends if you do whatever I command you.

  Jam 4:17 Therefore, to him who knows to do good and does not do it, to him it is sin.

  1Jn 2:5 But whoever keeps His word, truly the love of God is perfected in him. By this we know that we are in Him.

  2Jn 1:6a This is love, that we walk according to His commandments.

* **1Sam 15:22, 23a** Has the Lord as great delight in burnt offerings and sacrifices, As in obeying the voice of the Lord? Behold, to obey is better than sacrifice, And to heed than the fat of rams. For rebellion is as the sin of witchcraft, And stubbornness is as iniquity and idolatry.

Memorization of the Word

Memorizing the Word of God contributes greatly to the renewing of our mind. The more Word we have memorized, the more His truth will be in our heart. Promises stored in the heart are the fuel from which prayer receives life. The more you know God's Word, the more confidence you have in praying according to His Word.

By the same token the more you have his word hidden in your heart the more it will reflect in your witnessing. And using

III. THE LIVING WORD OF GOD

God's Word when speaking to others as the most effect in your ministering. Remember God's Word is an incorruptible seed. It will not return void of its fulfillment.

(At the end of this handbook we have added a section called "Memorization" which includes many of the verses that we must know either by heart or be very familiar with.)

Deut 11:18a Therefore you shall lay up these words of mine in your heart and in your soul.

Ps 40:8 I delight to do Your will, O my God, And Your law is within my heart.

Ps 119:129 Your testimonies are wonderful; Therefore my soul keeps them.

Ps 119:167 My soul keeps Your testimonies, and I love them exceedingly.

Pr 4:4 He also taught me, and said to me: let your heart retain my words; Keep my commands, and live.

Ps 119:11 Your word I have hidden in my heart, that I might not sin against You.

IV. LIVING A VIBRANT RELATIONSHIP WITH GOD IS THE ESSENCE OF THE NEW TESTAMENT

The Believer's Relationship with the Lord

God is our Father and He desires to have an intimate relationship with each one of us, His children. As a son or daughter we have been given the right to be in constant communication with Him. He has given us Jesus to redeem us for that purpose that we may be reunited. He wants our love and wants us to seek Him first.

To seek first means foremost and above all! Before everything else, above everything else, beyond everything else, and more than anything else! It means putting God first in our life. Our love for Him should be our first love.

Mt 22:37, 38 You shall love the Lord your God with all your heart, with all your soul, and with all your mind. This is the first and great commandment.

Deut 6:5 You shall love the Lord your God with all your heart, with all your soul, and with all your strength.

Jn 4:24 God is Spirit, and those who worship Him must worship in Spirit and truth.

Ps 34:1-3 I will bless the Lord at all times; His praise shall continually be in my mouth. My soul shall make its boast in the Lord; the humble shall hear of it and be glad. Oh, magnify the Lord with me, and let us exalt His name together.

Ps 63:1-4 O God, You are my God; Early will I seek You; My soul thirsts for You; my flesh longs for You In a dry and thirsty land where there is no water. So I have looked for You in the sanctuary, to see Your power and Your glory. Because Your lovingkindness is better than life, my lips shall praise You. Thus I will bless You while I live; I will lift up my hands in Your name.

IV. LIVING A VIBRANT RELATIONSHIP WITH GOD

Ps 73:25 Whom have I in heaven but You? And there is none upon earth that I desire besides You.

Ps 119:20 My soul breaks with longing for Your judgments at all times.

* **Pr 8:17** I love those who love Me, and those who seek Me early will find Me.

* **Jam 4:8a** Draw near to God and He will draw near to you.

2Cor 6:18 And I will be a Father unto you, and you will be My sons and daughters, saith the Lord Almighty.

Jn 17:21-23 That they may be one, as You, Father, are in Me, and I in You; that they also may be one in Us, that the world may believe that You sent Me. And the glory which You gave Me I have given them, that they may be one just as We are one. I in them, and You in Me; that they may be made perfect in one, and that the world may know that You have sent Me, and have loved them as You have loved Me.

* **Ps 73:25, 26** Whom have I in heaven but You? And there is none upon earth that I desire besides You. My flesh and my heart fails; but God is the strength of my heart and my portion forever.

* **Ro 7:4** Therefore, my brethren, you also have become dead to the law through the body of Christ, that you may be married to another–to Him who was raised from the dead, that we should bear fruit to God.

* **2Tim 1:12b** I know whom I have believed and am persuaded that He is able to keep what I have committed to Him until that Day.

How much God Loves Us

Jesus was the expression of God's love. God loves you so much that He sent Jesus on a mission of love with a message of love. The Bible doesn't say God has love; it says God is love. Love is His nature. He showed God's love, He symbolised God's love. He manifested God's love in every way for us. God loved us so perfectly, that He has sent His only Son to die in our stead.

He loves you regardless of whether or not you think you deserve His love. *"God loved the world so much. He gave His one and only Son, so that everyone who believes in Him will not perish but have eternal life" (John 3:16).* God made you so He could love you and so that you could love Him. His love for us is based upon His character and not on anything we do, say, or feel. Ephesians 3 says God's love is so wide, long, high, and deep that humans can't fully understand it.

1Jn 3:1 Behold what manner of love the Father has bestowed on us, that we should be called children of God! Therefore the world does not know us, because it did not know Him.

Jer 29:11 For I know the thoughts that I think toward you, says the Lord, thoughts of peace and not of evil, to give you a future and a hope.

Jer 31:3 I have loved you with an everlasting love; therefore with lovingkindness I have drawn you.

Isa 62:5b As the bridegroom rejoices over the bride, so shall your God rejoice over you.

* **Jn 14:23** If anyone loves Me, he will keep My word; and My Father will love him, and we will come to him and make our home with him.

Ro 5:8 But God demonstrates His own love toward us, in that while we were still sinners, Christ died for us.

Ro 8:17a And if children, then heirs—heirs of God and joint heirs with Christ.

* **Ro 8:38, 39** For I am persuaded that neither death nor life, nor angels nor principalities nor powers, nor things present nor things to come, nor height nor depth, nor any other created thing, shall be able to separate us from the love of God which is in Christ Jesus our Lord.

Gal 4:5-7 To redeem those who were under the law, that we might receive the adoption as sons. And because you are sons, God has sent forth the Spirit of His Son into your hearts, crying

IV. LIVING A VIBRANT RELATIONSHIP WITH GOD 50

out, Abba, Father. Therefore you are no longer a slave but a son, and if a son, then an heir of God through Christ.

1Jn 4:9 In this the love of God was manifested toward us, that God has sent His only begotten Son into the world, that we might live through Him.

* **1Jn 4:19** We love Him, because He first loved us.

Eph 3:16, 19 That He would grant you, according to the riches of His glory, to be strengthened with might through His Spirit in the inner man. To know the love of Christ which passes knowledge; that you may be filled with all the fullness of God.

* **Rev 3:20** Behold, I stand at the door and knock. If anyone hears My voice and opens the door, I will come in to him and dine
* with him, and he with Me.

Faith ~ the Only Way to Please God

Faith is more than a casual "I believe". Faith is a stance, a firm position, a conviction of the heart. Faith is not faith unless it's all you hang on to. It is akin to courage and standing up for what you believe. Faith is to believe what you don't see. The reward of faith is you get to see what you believed.

If you mix the Word of God with your faith and your voice, you will have an explosion of life and promises. The Lord loves you to remind Him of His Word, it shows you have faith in it. It's a positive declaration of your faith and your knowledge of the Word which pleases God! God has given us abundant promises in His Word, and when these promises are activated by our faith, God will always be true to His Word.

The promise, much like a seed, has power but you have to add water, your faith. Add faith to God's Word and you'll ignite the possibilities of God for you. *"Faith comes by hearing, and hearing by the Word of God" (Ro 10:17).* That second "hearing" in the above verse should be spelled "heeding". It's not the same word in the original Greek. The first word refers to <u>hearing</u>, but the second "hearing" in Greek refers to an action, as in heeding, doing.

Jesus made a clear distinction between those who <u>hear</u> only and those who <u>act</u> out their faith. He made it clear that unless you DO (heed, act on) the Word, your house will fall (Mt 7:24-27). And James said, *"Faith without works is dead"* (Jam 2:26). Faith has to be active to be alive. Faith is motion-activated. And it puts you in the right position to receive from God.

* **Heb 11:6** But without faith it is impossible to please Him, for he who comes to God must believe that He is, and that He is a rewarder of those who diligently seek Him.

* **Jam 2:26** For as the body without the spirit is dead, so faith without works is dead also.

   Heb 4:2b But the word which they heard did not profit them, not being mixed with faith in those who heard it.

* **Heb 11:1** Now faith is the substance of things hoped for, the evidence of things not seen.

* **Mt 9:29b** According to your faith let it be to you.

   Jn 20:27b Do not be unbelieving, but believing.

* **Ro 4:20, 21** He did not waver at the promises of God through unbelief, but was strong in faith, giving glory to God, and being fully convinced that what He had promised He was able to perform.

* **Ro 10:17** So then faith comes by hearing, and hearing by the Word of God.

   Ro 12:3b God has dealt to each one a measure of faith.

* **Ro 14:23b** Whatever is not from faith is sin.

* **2Cor 5:7** For we walk by faith, not by sight.

   2Cor 4:18 While we do not look at the things which are seen, but at the things which are not seen. For the things which are seen are temporary, but the things which are not seen are eternal.

   Heb 10:23 Let us hold fast the confession of our hope without wavering, for He who promised is faithful.

IV. LIVING A VIBRANT RELATIONSHIP WITH GOD

Heb 10:35 Therefore do not cast away your confidence, which has great reward.

Heb 10:38 Now the just shall live by faith; But if anyone draws back, My soul has no pleasure in him.

Heb 12:2 Looking unto Jesus, the author and finisher of our faith, who for the joy that was set before Him endured the cross, despising the shame, and has sat down at the right hand of the throne of God.

* **Jam 1:6-8** But let him ask in faith, with no doubting, for he who doubts is like a wave of the sea driven and tossed by the wind. For let not that man suppose that he will receive anything from the Lord; he is a double-minded man, unstable in all his ways.
* **2Tim 2:13** If we are faithless, He remains faithful; He cannot deny Himself.
* **1Jn 5:4** For whatever is born of God overcomes the world, and this is the victory that has overcomes the world, even our faith.
* **Job 13:15a** Though He slay me, yet will I trust Him.
* **Rev 3:11b** Holdfast what you have, that no one may take your crown.
* **Eph 5:16** Redeeming the time, because the days are evil.
* **Pr 3:5, 6** Trust in the Lord with all your heart, And lean not on your own understanding; In all your ways acknowledge Him, and He shall direct your paths.

Enduring Faith ~ God's Waiting Room

While faith on its own is most pleasing to God, when it pairs up with a few attributes, it gains strength. Faith gets tested when it doesn't see the answer or the manifestation immediately. Waiting is actually a good thing. A delay is not a denial. "No" is not the same as "not yet".

Delay is the test and the strength of faith because faith gathers momentum and strength in patience. Faith knows from the start that "whatever things you ask when you pray, believe that you receive them, and you will have them" (Mk 11:24). When faith pairs up with perseverance it turns into patience.

Genuine faith must be free of unbelief and rest its whole weight on God's promises, because it knows without a shadow of doubt that God will, as He promised. It can persevere because it keeps on believing till it gets the answer. It remains at rest. *"You will keep him in perfect peace, whose mind is stayed on you. Because he trusts in you" (Is 26:3).*

We think we have faith, but we never know the strength of our faith until we're tested. Faith cannot be head knowledge only. Many spiritual battles are lost in God's "waiting room" because that's where Satan is hard at work to cause us to doubt, waver and fear that the answer will not come. He tries to prove that God's Word doesn't work. But endurance is persistent faith. It is faith outlasting the devil. It is seeing the answer without looking back. We tend to pray for more faith, but it's not always faith that we need more of, but the other attributes of faith; insistence, endurance, patience, perseverance and trust.

When we understand how faith works, much like a seed planted in our heart, we can let it grow towards the promised blessings as it develops into the different stages of its growth. Once planted in our heart, faith will turn to perseverance and it then turns to endurance and then to patience and then to trust, much like a seed morphs into different forms as it grows. "First the seed, then the blade, then the corn" (Mk 4:28). All that takes time.

But all throughout its morphing process, faith continues to reflect brightness in its expectancy, much like an expectant mother. She counts it done! The longer the wait, the larger the expectancy. Faith has that same expectant smile.

If you are going to rejoice when you get the answer, why not start rejoicing now. You can start praising even in the waiting room. Praise has the power to speak the desired request into existence "as though they were" (Ro 4:17). That's why it is important after we pray never to doubt, never to say, "Oh well, it didn't work." You have to leave that seed in the ground for it to do its work, and trust the power of the seed to produce its fruit.

IV. LIVING A VIBRANT RELATIONSHIP WITH GOD

We all know how hard it is to "wait on the Lord". However, once we understand how faith grows and develops, it is easier to understand the waiting room of God. Many saints have spent time in God's waiting room; Joseph (13 years), Abraham (100 years), Moses (40 years). God does not work on the same timetable as we do, but God does keep His promises. He has staked His reputation on them.

Waiting is an essential part of faith. In the book of Hebrews it says, "All these obtained a good report through faith" (Heb 11:2), even though they didn't get to actually see the promise. But because they never doubted that God would answer, they did receive the promise nonetheless. The key to persevering faith is to act as if the answer is already here while you wait.

Faith is increased thru patience. It is like in exercising, much like a muscle, it is nourished by sore trials. It's the trial of your faith that works patience in you. *"That the trial of your faith being more precious than gold, that you might obtain praise, honor and glory" (Ja 1:3; 1Pt 1:7)*. The Bible says, *"He that wavers, let not that man think that he will receive anything of the Lord" (Heb 11:6)*.

Doubt has no place in faith because "without (unwavering) faith, it is impossible to please God". Enduring faith shows God that you trust Him. Trust is a firm belief rooted in love and that is where God is most pleased, when we're willing to trust Him.

Trust is faith tested through patience. It is that inner conviction which transforms the substance of hope into the reality of possession. *"Now faith is the substance of things hoped for, the evidence of things not seen"(Heb 11:1)*. Mountains of difficulties, hindrances and doubts can be moved out of the way by trust's persistent faith and virile perseverance. That's when we see the manifestation of our requests. Remember what Jesus said to Thomas, *"Because you have seen Me, you have believed. But more blessed are those who have not seen, and have believed" (Jn 20:29)*.

Ro 12:12 Rejoicing in hope, patient in tribulation, continuing steadfastly in prayer.

Ps 31:15 My times are in Your hand; Deliver me from the hand of my enemies, And from those who persecute me.

Ps 130:5 I wait for the Lord, my soul waits, and in His word I do hope.

* **Gal 6:9** And let us not grow weary while doing good, for in due season we shall reap if we do not lose heart.

Ps 27:14 Wait on the Lord; Be of good courage, and He shall strengthen your heart; Wait, I say, on the Lord!

Ps 30:5b Weeping may endure for a night, but joy comes in the morning.

Mt 24:13 But he who endures to the end shall be saved.

Ro 8:24 For we were saved in this hope, but hope that is seen is not hope; for why does one still hope for what he sees? But if we hope for what we do not see, we eagerly wait for it with perseverance. Likewise the Spirit also helps in our weaknesses.

Ro 5:2-4 Through whom we have gained access by faith into this grace in which we now stand. And we boast in the hope of the glory of God. Not only so, but we also glory in our sufferings, because we know that suffering produces perseverance; perseverance, character; and character, hope.

Ecc 7:8 The end of a thing is better than its beginning; The patient in spirit is better than the proud in spirit.

Ps 18:30 As for God, His way is perfect; The word of the Lord is proven; He is a shield to all who trust in Him.

Ps 27:14 Wait on the Lord; Be of good courage, And He shall strengthen your heart; Wait, I say, on the Lord!

Jam 5:7-8 Therefore be patient, brethren, until the coming of the Lord. See how the farmer waits for the precious fruit of the earth, waiting patiently for it until it receives the early and latter rain. You also be patient. Establish your hearts, for the coming of the Lord]is at hand.

Ps 130:5 I wait for the Lord, my soul waits, And in His word I do hope.

Lam 3:24-26 The Lord is my portion," says my soul, "Therefore I hope in Him!" The Lord is good to those who wait for Him, To the soul who seeks Him. It is good that one should hope and wait quietly For the salvation of the Lord.

Believers are Given the Full Authority of Christ

Because through Jesus we have been made sons of God, we are now partakers of the same inheritance as Jesus had, including the same authority and power as Jesus has, to bring God's will on earth as it is in heaven, and to destroy the works of the devil. He lives in us, and it's His power working through us. We have been given His name to use in order to operate here on earth in His stead, and in His authority.

1Jn 3:8b For this purpose the Son of God was manifested, that He might destroy the works of the devil.

Mt 16:19 And I will give you the keys of the kingdom of heaven, and whatever you bind on earth will be bound in heaven, and whatever you loose on earth will be loosed in heaven.

* **Lk 1:37** For with God nothing will be impossible.

Lk 18:27 The things which are impossible with men are possible with God.

* **Jn 15:7** If you abide in Me, and My words abide in you, you will ask what you desire, and it shall be done for you.

Mt 28:18b All authority has been given to Me in heaven and on earth.

Jn 14:12, 13 Most assuredly, I say to you, he who believes in Me, the works that I do he will do also; and greater works than these he will do, because I go to My Father. And whatever you ask in My name, that I will do, that the Father may be glorified in the Son.

Gen 1:26 Then God said, "Let Us make man in Our image, according to Our likeness; let them have dominion over the fish of the sea, over the birds of the air, and over the cattle, over all the earth and over every creeping thing that creeps on the earth".

Ps 8:6 You have made him to have dominion over the works of Your hands; you have put all things under his feet.

* **Mk 9:23** If you can believe, all things are possible to him who believes.

Jn 16:23, 24 Most assuredly, I say to you, whatever you ask the Father in My name He will give you. Until now you have asked nothing in My name. Ask, and you will receive, that your joy may be full.

Eph 1:19-22 And what is the exceeding greatness of His power toward us who believe, according to the working of His mighty power which He worked in Christ when He raised Him from the dead and seated Him at His right hand in the heavenly places, far above all principality and power and might and dominion, and every name that is named, not only in this age, but also in that which is to come. And He put all things under His feet, and gave Him to be head over all things to the church.

* **Eph 3:20** Now to Him who is able to do exceedingly abundantly above all that we ask or think, according to the power that works in us.

Phil 2:9-11 Therefore God also has highly exalted Him and given Him the name which is above every name, that at the name of Jesus every knee should bow, of those in heaven, and of those on earth, and of those under the earth, and that every tongue should confess that Jesus Christ is Lord, to the glory of God the Father.

Honoring the Lord in all of Our Ways

Honoring God is to <u>revere</u> Him, or what the Bible calls "fearing God", <u>reverencing</u> Him for all He is; for His goodness and His awesomeness. Therefore, we are to <u>fear</u> and <u>honor</u> Him as our Father, our Creator, our God; the <u>only</u> and the <u>almighty</u> God.

IV. LIVING A VIBRANT RELATIONSHIP WITH GOD

Deut 10:12b What does the Lord your God require of you, but to fear the Lord your God, to walk in all His ways and to love Him, to serve the Lord your God with all your heart and with all your soul.

1Sam 12:24 Only fear the Lord, and serve Him in truth with all your heart; for consider what great things He has done for you.

Ps 25:14 The secret of the Lord is with those who fear Him, and He will show them His covenant.

Ps 31:19a Oh, how great is Your goodness which You have laid up for those who fear You.

Ps 103:11 For as the heavens are high above the earth, so great is His mercy toward those who fear Him.

* **Ps 111:10a** The fear of the Lord is the beginning of wisdom.

Ps 147:11 The Lord takes pleasure in those who fear Him, in those who hope in His mercy.

Pr 1:7a The fear of the Lord is the beginning of knowledge.

Pr 8:13a The fear of the Lord is to hate evil.

Pr 14:26, 27 In the fear of the Lord there is strong confidence. The fear of the Lord is a fountain of life.

Lk 1:50 And His mercy is on those who fear Him from generation to generation.

Acts 10:35 But in every nation whoever fears Him and works righteousness is accepted by Him.

Resting in the Lord ~ The True Sabbath

We all need more quiet time alone with the Lord in rest and refilling. The secret of that calm and peace and rest and patience and trust is resting in the Lord. No work is too important to stop for a few minutes of inspiration and refreshing from on high, spiritual renewal and physical rest, a little love feast with the Lord. He can solve all your problems in one little glimpse. He can refresh your whole spirit with one deep breath. He can clarify all your thoughts with just one sweet strain of heavenly music! He can wipe away all your fears and tears with just one little restful moment in the perfect peace that He gives when your mind is stayed on Him and Him alone because you trust Him! Strength comes from the Lord who made heaven and earth (Ps 121:1, 2) and your body, and He knows what you need most of all! Rest and peace and fellowship with Him and feeding on His Word.

* **Mt 11:28-30** Come to Me, all you who labor and are heavy laden, and I will give you rest. Take My yoke upon you and learn from Me, for I am gentle and lowly in heart, and you will find rest for your souls. For My yoke is easy and My burden is light.

Ps 23:2, 3a He makes me to lie down in green pastures; He leads me beside the still waters. He restores my soul.

Ps 46:10a Be still, and know that I am God.

Ps 37:7a Rest in the Lord, and wait patiently for Him.

Isa 30:7b Their strength is to sit still.

Isa 30:15 For thus says the Lord God, the Holy One of Israel: In returning and rest you shall be saved; in quietness and confidence shall be your strength.

Isa 40:29-31 He gives power to the weak, and to those who have no might He increases strength. Even the youths shall faint and be weary, and the young men shall utterly fall. But those who wait on the Lord shall renew their strength; they shall mount up with wings like eagles. They shall run and not be weary. They shall walk and not faint.

Heb 4:9-11a There remains therefore a rest for the people of God. For he who has entered His rest has himself also ceased from his works as God did from His. Let us therefore be diligent to enter that rest.

2Cor 4:16b Even though our outward *man* is perishing, yet the inward man is being renewed day by day.

Jer 31:25 For I have satiated the weary soul, and I have replenished every sorrowful soul.

Mk 2:27 And He said to them, "The Sabbath was made for man, not man for the Sabbath."

Ex 33:14 And He said, "My presence will go with you, and I will give you rest."

V. PRAYER: THE BELIEVER'S DIRECT LINE TO GOD

The understanding of the authority given back to the born again man is what gives meaning to prayer. In prayer, we are to enforce on earth the laws of God's kingdom, as it is in heaven. The world we live in is no longer trapped by its limitations; the born again man was given back power and authority over those limitations to rule in life! Rulership, dominion, victory, triumph, and conquest is what Jesus paid for. We are promised a winning life if we're willing to fight for it.

Christians are to enforce the victory of the cross and that's where we start in our prayer life. Through His resurrection, Jesus has loosed a force that has restructured the spirit world and prayer opens the way to that dynamic victory and shakes and shatters the world of darkness.

Prayer shouldn't be a begging session with God. Knowing that He's promised to provide all our needs, doesn't require us to beg Him, but rather to thank Him for His many promises. God has supplied everything through His grace, so prayer takes on a new meaning. In many respects, we are not to beg God for anything that He has already done and provided through His grace, but rather thank Him. And as for anything that He's already given us the responsibility and authority to do, we are to <u>command</u> those things to be. While we must see prayer as war, we are not fighting against nor begging God, but we are in violent interference against the oppressor.

The god of this world has been dethroned by the Son of God and we are the enforcers of that victory. The freed have become the free-ers.

Prayer is one of the means God has chosen to work through us. In the book of Acts, every invasion of God's people with the message of the gospel was always preceded by prayer. Prayer is reclaiming the kingdom of heaven by force, *"And the violent take it by force" (Mat 11:12b)*. Prayer oftentimes requires wrestling. We often have to put our shoulder to the boulder in persistence and perseverance until we get the answer. Faith doesn't ever give up; or else it isn't genuine faith. Faith has the ability to see the end from the beginning and it never lets go.

The devil fights a praying man most because he knows that God has hardwired the universe to work through prayer when He said, *"Ask and you shall receive" (Mat 7:7)*. It is the prayer of faith that brings the end of impossible before us.

We sometimes tend to use prayer as our last resort, but it ought to be our first line of offense. We ought not to resort to prayer because there's nothing else we can do, but we ought to pray before we do anything else. *"Everyone that asks receives" (Mat 7:8)*. That's the childlike faith that we ought to have. Faith is the fuel of prayer and it brings us before the omnipotence of God. God holds Himself ready to supply exactly and fully all the demands of faith in prayer. *"He will have whatsoever he says" (Mk 11:23)*.

The keynote of prayer is "have faith in God" for *"he that comes to God must believe that He is and that He is the rewarder of those who diligently seek Him" (Heb 11:6)*. Prayer is made strong by the Word. Again, God loves for you to remind Him of His promises because it proves your trust in His Word.

God Hears and Answers Every Prayer

Jesus said, *"All things, whatsoever you shall ask in prayer, believing, you shall receive" (Mt 21:22)*. Jesus is saying that having faith is the key to receiving answers to prayer! God has confined Himself and His operations to our faith and our prayers in the name of Jesus. (See Jn 14:13)

* **Heb 11:6** But without faith it is impossible to please Him, for he who comes to God must believe that He is, and that He is a rewarder of those who diligently seek Him.

Jam 5:16b The effective, fervent prayer of a righteous man avails much.

Ps 116:1, 2 I love the Lord, because He has heard My voice and my supplications. Because He has inclined His ear to me, therefore I will call upon Him as long as I live.

2Sam 22:7 In my distress I called upon the Lord, and cried out to my God; He heard my voice from His temple, and my cry entered His ears.

Isa 30:19b He will be very gracious to you at the sound of your cry; when He hears it, He will answer you.

* **Isa 65:24** It shall come to pass that before they call, I will answer; and while they are still speaking, I will hear.

* **Jer 33:3** Call to Me, and I will answer you, and show you great and mighty things, which you do not know.

Ps 50:15 Call upon Me in the day of trouble; I will deliver you, and you shall glorify Me.

Ps 91:15a He shall call upon Me, and I will answer him.

Mt 6:6b But you, when you pray, go into your room, and when you have shut your door, pray to your Father who is in the secret place; and your Father who sees in secret will reward you openly.

* **Mt 7:7, 8** Ask, and it will be given to you; seek, and you will find; knock, and it will be opened to you. For everyone who asks receives, and he who seeks finds, and to him who knocks it will be opened.

* **Jn 15:7** If you abide in Me, and My words abide in you, you will ask what you desire, and it shall be done for you.

Ro 8:34 It is Christ who died, and furthermore is also risen, who is even at the right hand of God, who also makes intercession for us.

Ps 22:24 For He has not despised nor abhorred the affliction of the afflicted; nor has He hidden His face from Him; but when He cried to Him, He heard.

Ps 55:17 Evening and morning and at noon I will pray, and cry aloud, and He shall hear my voice.

Ps 62:8 Trust in Him at all times, you people; pour out your heart before Him; God is a refuge for us.

V. PRAYER: THE BELIEVER'S DIRECT LINE TO GOD

Ps 102:17 He shall regard the prayer of the destitute, and shall not despise their prayer.

Ps 119:10 With my whole heart I have sought You; oh, let me not wander from Your commandments!

Lam 2:19a Arise, cry out in the night, at the beginning of the watches; pour out your heart like water before the face of the Lord.

* **Jer 29:13** And you will seek Me and find Me, when you search for Me with all your heart.
* **Jn 14:14** If you ask anything in My name, I will do it
* **Heb 4:16** Let us therefore come boldly to the throne of grace, that we may obtain mercy and find grace to help in time of need.
* **1Thes 5:17** Pray without ceasing.
* **1Jn 5:14, 15** Now this is the confidence that we have in Him, that if we ask anything according to His will, He hears us. And if we know that He hears us, whatever we ask, we know that we have the petitions that we have asked of Him.
* **Isa 45:11b** Ask Me of things to come concerning My sons; and concerning the work of My hands, you command Me.
* **Ps 66:18, 19** If I regard iniquity in my heart, the Lord will not hear. But certainly God has heard me; He has attended to the voice of my prayer.
* **Mt 18:19, 20** If two of you agree on earth concerning anything that they ask, it will be done for them by My Father in heaven. For where two or three are gathered together in My name, I am there in the midst of them.
* **Ro 8:26** Likewise the Spirit also helps in our weaknesses. For we do not know what we should pray for as we ought, but the Spirit Himself makes intercession for us with groanings which cannot be uttered.

Pray in Faith, Fully Believing

Our faith is what brings the answers from the eternal to the present. Believing is not a light matter, it is a solid and immovable stance. It is not only an expectation, but a firm assertion, as certain as a cashed check at the bank. Faith goes boldly against the impossible to validate God's Word! Faith fully depends on His promises!

* **Mk 11:24** Therefore I say to you, whatever things you ask when you pray, believe that you receive them, and you will have them.

Jam 1:6-7 But let him ask in faith, with no doubting, for he who doubts is like a wave of the sea driven and tossed by the wind. For let not that man suppose that he will receive anything from the Lord.

Ro 4:21 And being fully convinced that what He had promised He was also able to perform.

Mt 21:21-22 Jesus answered and said to them, "Assuredly, I say to you, if you have faith and do not doubt, you will not only do what was done to the fig tree, but also if you say to this mountain, 'Be removed and be cast into the sea,' it will be done. And whatever things you ask in prayer, believing, you will receive."

Lk 11:9-10 So I say to you, ask, and it will be given to you; seek, and you will find; knock, and it will be opened to you. For everyone who asks receives, and he who seeks finds, and to him who knocks it will be opened.

Heb 7:25 Therefore He is also able to save to the uttermost those who come to God through Him, since He always lives to make intercession for them.

* **1Jn 3:22** Whatever we ask we receive from Him, because we keep His commandments and do those things that are pleasing in His sight.

Praising and Worshiping God

There is so much power in praise and worship! The psalmist, David, continually sang praises to God! In Psalm 22:3, David says that God dwells, or inhabits our praises! Praise honors God for His presence, His power, His goodness, His creation and His love for us! When we praise God, we are not only glorifying Him, but our praises lift us above difficult circumstances and into the goodness of God. We then see from God's perspective, His possibilities and opportunities. Praise will often get us out of the pit in which the devil is trying to cast us! Even wars have been won through praising God, through praising His power and might (2Cor 20:22)!

Christians should not live a silent life. Praising expresses the testimonies of God. This is the reason we should not keep our praise to ourselves, but should praise out loud, extolling all His benefits and counting our blessings all ways. *"The Lord is worthy to be praised" (Ps 18:3)*. The spirit of praise is a mighty force in projecting the gospel. Praise destroys the atmosphere of the ill circumstances and lifts us into the perspective of God.

The book of Psalms is filled with praise and thankfulness, because thanksgiving is the oral, positive and active expression of gratitude. The Lord loves a praiseful and thankful heart, because gratitude is the inward emotion of the heart which meditates on God's grace and mercy; that is why the Lord abhors murmuring and complaining (1 Cor 10:10). All throughout the Bible we are admonished to praise and to be grateful in all things; to sing songs of thanksgiving, to rejoice evermore, to give thanks in everything.

Singing from a thankful heart also is a mighty way to express praise. Singing the praises of God has nothing to do with musical taste or talent, but with the rejoicing of the heart. It's His glorious presence which propels the singing and fills the notes of praise. Our lips should overflow out of the abundance of a heart of praise.

Praise has so many benefits: it magnifies the Lord in our mind and in our heart, it expands our vision and takes the limits off of God. It eclipses fear when we see God so big and so capable.

It energizes our work almost as if it gets done without us. It refreshes our spirit because it lifts us above the circumstances. Plus, Satan is defeated when we give God glory and praise. And lastly it prepares us for the heavenly, having known how to honor and revere God.

2Chr 20:22 Now when they began to sing and to praise, the Lord set ambushes against the people of Ammon, Moab, and Mount Seir, who had come against Judah; and they were defeated.

Jonah 2:9a But I will sacrifice to You with the voice of thanksgiving.

Ps 5:11 But let all those rejoice who put their trust in You; let them ever shout for joy, because You defend them; let those also who love Your name be joyful in You.

Ps 16:11b In Your presence is fullness of joy; at Your right hand are pleasures forevermore.

Ps 32:11 Be glad in the Lord and rejoice, you righteous; and shout for joy, all you upright in heart!

Ps 33:1 Rejoice in the Lord, O you righteous! For praise from the upright is beautiful.

* **Ps 34:1** I will bless the Lord at all times; His praise shall continually be in my mouth.

* **Ps 35:28** And my tongue shall speak of Your righteousness and of Your praise all the day long.

Ps 50:23 Whoever offers praise glorifies Me; And to him who orders his conduct aright I will show the salvation of God.

Ps 68:19 Blessed be the Lord, Who daily loads us with benefits, the God of our salvation.

Ps 71:8 Let my mouth be filled with Your praise and with Your glory all the day.

Ps 71:14 But I will hope continually, and will praise You yet more and more.

Ps 89:15 Blessed are the people who know the joyful sound! They walk, O Lord, in the light of Your countenance.

V. PRAYER: THE BELIEVER'S DIRECT LINE TO GOD

Ps 92:1, 2 It is good to give thanks to the Lord, and to sing praises to Your name, O Most High; to declare Your lovingkindness in the morning, and Your faithfulness every night.

Ps 100:4 Enter into His gates with thanksgiving, and into His courts with praise. Be thankful to Him, and bless His name.

Ps 103:1, 2 Bless the Lord, O my soul; and all that is within me, bless His holy name! Bless the Lord, O my soul, and forget not all His benefits.

* **Ps 107:8** Oh, that men would give thanks to the Lord for His goodness, and for His wonderful works to the children of men.

Ps 107:22 Let them sacrifice the sacrifices of thanksgiving, and declare His works with rejoicing.

Ps 113:3 From the rising of the sun to its going down the Lord's name is to be praised.

Ps 147:1 Praise the Lord! For it is good to sing praises to our God; for it is pleasant, and praise is beautiful.

Ps 150:6 Let everything that has breath praise the Lord. Praise the Lord!

Eph 5:19, 20 Speaking to one another in psalms and hymns and spiritual songs, singing and making melody in your heart to the Lord, giving thanks always for all things to God the Father in the name of our Lord Jesus Christ.

* **1Thes 5:16-18** Rejoice always, pray without ceasing, in everything give thanks; for this is the will of God in Christ Jesus for you.

* **Phil 4:6, 8** Be anxious for nothing, but in everything by prayer and supplication, with thanksgiving, let your requests be made known to God. Finally, brethren, whatever things are true, whatever things are noble, whatever things are just, whatever things are pure, whatever things are lovely, whatever things are of good report, if there is any virtue and if there is anything praiseworthy—meditate on these things.

Heb 13:15 Therefore by Him let us continually offer the sacrifice of praise to God, that is, the fruit of our lips, giving thanks to His name.

Rev 19:5b Praise our God, all you His servants and those who fear Him, both small and great.

* **Mt 18:18** Assuredly, I say to you, whatever you bind on earth will be bound in heaven, and whatever you loose on earth will be loosed in heaven.

***Eph 3:20** Now to Him who is able to do exceedingly abundantly above all that we ask or think, according to the power that works in us.

VI. DISCIPLESHIP MEANS "WALKING OUT" YOUR FAITH

What it Means to be a Christian Disciple

A Christian disciple is one who learns from, follows and lives like his Master, Jesus! Jesus said that if we love Him, we will keep His commandments (Jn 14:15) and that those who do His will (Mt 7:21) will enter into the kingdom! When we <u>walk</u> like Jesus walked, our actions, desires, motives and goals change to be in line with His Word and with His will for ourselves and for others.

Christian discipleship is a full departure from living as the world lives, it is a new lifestyle! Jesus prayed, *"I do not pray that You should take them out of the world, but that You should keep them from the evil one. They are not of the world, just as I am not of the world" (Jn 17:15, 16)*. In surrendering our life to Him, we let Him live <u>through</u> us.

Our life is no longer our own. Jesus said, *"If any man will come after Me, let him deny himself" (Mt 16:24)*. It's not only a sacrifice to live the Christian life, it's a full <u>denial</u> of oneself so that <u>He</u> may <u>live through</u> us. The Apostle Paul said, *"I am crucified with Christ, it is no longer I who live, but Christ lives in me" (Gal 2:20)*. The life of a Christian disciple involves a total commitment to following Jesus in order to be a <u>doer</u> of the Word and not a hearer only.

VI. DISCIPLESHIP MEANS "WALKING OUT" YOUR FAITH

We are not only students of God's Word, but followers of the discipline of Christ; meaning that we are practicing and living out His teachings. To be a disciple of Jesus is not only adhering to a set of beliefs, but a lifestyle.

Mt 7:24-27 Therefore, whoever hears these sayings of Mine, and <u>does</u> them, I will liken him to a wise man who built his house on the <u>rock</u>: and the floods came, and the winds blew and beat on that house; and it did not fall for it was founded on the rock. But everyone who hears these sayings of Mine, and <u>does not do them</u>, will be like a foolish man who built his house on the <u>sand</u>: and the rain descended, the floods came, and the winds blew and beat on that house, and it fell. And great was its fall.

Mt 16:24, 25 Then Jesus said to His disciples, "If anyone desires to come after Me, let him deny himself, and take up his cross, and follow Me. For whoever desires to save his life will lose it, but whoever loses his life for My sake will find it.

Jn 12:24 Most assuredly, I say to you, unless a grain of wheat falls into the ground and dies, it remains alone; but if it dies, it produces much grain.

Jn 12:25 He who loves his life will lose it, and he who hates his life in this world will keep it for eternal life.

Gal 2:20 I have been crucified with Christ; it is no longer I who live, but Christ lives in me; and the life which I now live in the flesh I live by faith in the Son of God, who loved me and gave Himself for me.

Jam 1:22-25 But be doers of the Word, and not hearers only, deceiving yourselves. For if anyone is a hearer of the word and not a doer, he is like a man observing his natural face in a mirror; for he observes himself, goes away, and immediately forgets what kind of man he was. But he who looks into the perfect law of liberty and continues in it, and is not a forgetful hearer, but a doer of the work, this one will be blessed in what he does.

* **Jn 8:31b, 32** If you abide in My Word, you are My disciples indeed. And you shall know the truth, and the truth shall make you free.

* **Lk 14:33** So likewise, whoever of you does not forsake all that he has cannot be My disciple.

* **Jn 13:35** By this all will know that you are My disciples, if you have love for one another.

* **Mt 6:24** No one can serve two masters; for either he will hate the one and love the other, or else he will be loyal to the one and despise the other. You cannot serve God and mammon.

* **Mt 10:36-38** A man's enemies will be those of his own household. He who loves father or mother more than Me is not worthy of Me. And he who loves son or daughter more than Me is not worthy of Me. And he who does not take his cross and follow after Me is not worthy of Me.

* **Mt 19:29** Everyone who has left houses or brothers or sisters or father or mother or wife or children or lands, for My name's sake, shall receive a hundredfold, and inherit eternal life.

   Mk 10:21 Then Jesus, looking at him, loved him, and said to him, "One thing you lack: Go your way, sell whatever you have and give to the poor, and you will have treasure in heaven; and come, take up the cross, and follow Me".

* **Lk 9:62** No one, having put his hand to the plow, and looking back, is fit for the kingdom of God.

* **1Cor 6:20** For you were bought at a price; therefore glorify God in your body and in your spirit, which are God's.

   2Cor 5:14a For the love of Christ compels us.

* **Phil 1:29** For to you it has been granted on behalf of Christ, not only to believe in Him, but also to suffer for His sake.

   Phil 3:7, 8 But what things were gain to me, these I have counted loss for Christ. Yet indeed I also count all things loss for the excellence of the knowledge of Christ Jesus my Lord, for

VI. DISCIPLESHIP MEANS "WALKING OUT" YOUR FAITH

whom I have suffered the loss of all things, and count them as rubbish, that I may gain Christ.

* **Eph 6:6** Not with eye service, as men-pleasers, but as bondservants of Christ, doing the will of God from the heart.
* **2Tim 2:3** You therefore must endure hardship as a good soldier of Jesus Christ.

  1Pt 2:9 But you are a chosen generation, a royal priesthood, a holy nation, His own special people, that you may proclaim the praises of Him who called you out of darkness into His marvelous light.
* **Lk 9:23-24** Then He said to them all, "If anyone desires to come after Me, let him deny himself, and take up his cross daily, and follow Me. For whoever desires to save his life will lose it, but whoever loses his life for My sake will save it.
* **Mt 22:14** For many are called, but few are chosen.
* **1Cor 11:1** Imitate me, just as I also imitate Christ.
* **Mt 23:11** But he who is greatest among you shall be your servant.
* **Heb 13:17** Obey those who rule over you, and be submissive, for they watch out for your souls, as those who must give account. Let them do so with joy and not with grief, for that would be unprofitable for you.
* **Pr 27:23** Be diligent to know the state of your flocks, and attend to your herds.
* **Pr 11:14** Where there is no guidance the people fall, but in abundance of counselors there is victory.
* **Jn 15:16** You did not choose Me, but I chose you and appointed you that you should go and bear fruit, and that your fruit should remain, that whatever you ask the Father in My name He may give you.
* **Mt 9:37, 38** Then He said to His disciples, "The harvest truly is plentiful, but the laborers are few. Therefore pray the Lord of the harvest to send out laborers into His harvest."

Christians must Bear Fruit

Jesus said, "By this My Father is glorified, that you bear much fruit; so you will be My disciples" (Jn 15:8). Jesus glorified the Father by bearing fruit in every walk of His life. He preached the good news, He healed the sick, cast out devils and raised the dead!

He was bringing the kingdom of God to earth in everything He did! For us to bear fruit for the kingdom of God, as Jesus did, we "receive the seed (the Word of God) into good ground (which is hearing the Word and understanding it), and we will bear fruit in different measures (Mt 13:23). Plus, God has given each one of us gifts and talents to use for His glory. Some of us are good at art, others at sport, and yet others at finances, etc. God shaped all of us differently and He takes pleasure in seeing us use the gifts and the talents He's given us.

We don't have to always be doing something "spiritual" to bring God glory. Any time we're using our gifts for His glory, it's pleasing to Him. The keyword is to <u>use</u> those gifts and bear fruit unto Him. Some gifts are spiritual while others are physical, but all can be developed and used to bring Him glory. Remember the parable of the talents. He was most pleased with those that <u>used</u> and grew their talents and disappointed in the one who did nothing with his talents.

* **Jn 15:8** By this My Father is glorified, that you bear much fruit; so you will be My disciples.

Mt 5:14-16 You are the light of the world. A city that is set on a hill cannot be hidden. Nor do they light a lamp and put it under a basket, but on a lampstand, and it gives light to all who are in the house. Let your light so shine before men, that they may see your good works and glorify your Father in heaven.

Ro 7:4 Therefore, my brethren, you also have become dead to the law through the body of Christ, that you may be married to another—to Him who was raised from the dead, that we should bear fruit to God.

VI. DISCIPLESHIP MEANS "WALKING OUT" YOUR FAITH

* **Ps 1:3** He shall be like a tree planted by the rivers of water, that brings forth its fruit in its season, whose leaf also shall not wither; and whatever he does shall prosper.
* **Mt 7:18, 20** A good tree cannot bear bad fruit, nor can a bad tree bear good fruit. Every tree that does not bear good fruit is cut down and thrown into the fire. Therefore by their fruits you will know them.

Mt 25:34-40 Then the King will say to those on His right hand, 'Come, you blessed of My Father, inherit the kingdom prepared for you from the foundation of the world: for I was hungry and you gave Me food; I was thirsty and you gave Me drink; I was a stranger and you took Me in; I was naked and you clothed Me; I was sick and you visited Me; I was in prison and you came to Me. Then the righteous will answer Him, saying, 'Lord, when did we see You hungry and feed You, or thirsty and give You drink? When did we see You a stranger and take You in, or naked and clothe You? Or when did we see You sick, or in prison, and come to You?' And the King will answer and say to them, 'Assuredly, I say to you, inasmuch as you did it to one of the least of these My brethren, you did it to Me.'

Mk 4:8 But other seed fell on good ground and yielded a crop that sprang up, increased and produced: some thirtyfold, some sixty, and some a hundred.

* **Jn 6:27** Do not labor for the food which perishes, but for the food which endures to everlasting life, which the Son of Man will give you, because God the Father has set His seal on Him.
* **Jn 12:24** Unless a grain of wheat falls into the ground and dies, it remains alone; but if it dies, it produces much grain.
* **Heb 11:15, 16** And truly if they had called to mind that country from which they had come out, they would have had opportunity to return. But now they desire a better, that is, a heavenly country. Therefore, God is not ashamed to be called their God, for He has prepared a city for them.

Jn 15:4, 5 Abide in Me, and I in you. As the branch cannot bear fruit of itself, unless it abides in the vine, neither can you, unless you abide in Me. I am the vine, you are the branches. He who abides in Me, and I in him, bears much fruit; for without Me you can do nothing.

The Christian's Relationship to the World

Is it even worth it to be a Christian? For one, it isn't easy to live for Christ in a world that doesn't like Christ. Wouldn't it be easier to just live a life of ease and enjoy the comforts of life like everyone else does? Why deny yourself and your own life while others are enjoying theirs?

Paul said, *"If our hope in Christ is good for this life only and no more, then we, Christians, deserve more pity than anyone else in all the world" (1 Cor 15:19)*. Paul was no dummy as far as the world is concerned. He was highly educated and had just about every degree from Bible colleges than anyone could have in those days. And then he said, *"I once thought these things were valuable, but now I consider them worthless because of what Christ has done. Yes, everything else is worthless when compared with the infinite value of knowing Christ Jesus my Lord. For His sake I have discarded everything else, counting it all as garbage, so that I could gain Christ" (Phil 3:7-8)*.

Why count it all worthless and forsake it all? Because of what Jesus said: *"For what profit is it to a man if he gains the whole world, and loses his own soul? Or what will a man give in exchange for his soul?" (Mat 16:26)*. Some people trade their souls for worldly things, like money, fame, good looks and materialism. That's the price of compromise.

Jesus had a lot to say about compromise. *"For whoever is ashamed of Me and My words in this adulterous and sinful generation, of him the Son of Man also will be ashamed when He comes in the glory of His Father with the holy angels" (Mk 8:38)*. We have to make that choice, whether to stay true and be all-in for the message and doctrine of Jesus and preaching it and practicing it, or choose safety, comfort, convenience, compromise, peace and support.

VI. DISCIPLESHIP MEANS "WALKING OUT" YOUR FAITH

It is important that people know what we stand for; it is equally important that they know what we won't stand for. He who tolerates evil without protesting against it is really cooperating with it. Everything in life has a price tag. Anytime we say yes to something, we're saying no to something else. Is the prize of your soul worth the price of following Christ? Compromise may be one of the greatest challenges for Christians. The most uncomfortable place for a Christian is a comfortable one. We must always watch out about any compromise or pulling our punches for advantage, for popularity or for finances, for protection, for safety, for anything. Thomas Carlyle said, "Conviction is worthless unless it is converted into conduct."

Real, meaningful success isn't based on what you accumulate, or your appearance, or feeling good. Real success comes from living your life by real values; by God's values for which we were created. The apostle Paul realized that no status, no amount of money, no fame nor fortune, no earthly pleasure is worth more than Jesus.

Once we are born again, we become a part of the kingdom of light, and we are no longer a part of the kingdom of darkness. (Col 1:12-13). So why should we desire again "fellowship with the works of darkness"? There should be quite a few very noticeable changes in our lives. The more we study and meditate on the Word of God, the more He changes our habits, our desires, our goals, and even those we fellowship with. Certain former pleasures, acquaintances and even former habits are no longer appealing. This is why we vehemently discipline ourselves to renew our minds and actions to be in accordance with our new life and identity in Christ.

* **Gal 5:1** Stand fast therefore in the liberty by which Christ has made us free, and do not be entangled again with a yoke of bondage.
* **Eph 5:11** And have no fellowship with the unfruitful works of darkness, but rather expose them.

Mt 7:13 Enter by the narrow gate; for wide is the gate and broad is the way that leads to destruction, and there are many who go in by it.

Ro 6:12 Therefore do not let sin reign in your mortal body, that you should obey it in its lusts.

* **2Cor 6:14** Do not be unequally yoked together with unbelievers. For what fellowship has righteousness with lawlessness? And what communion has light with darkness?

* **2Cor 6:17** "Come out from among them and be separate", says the Lord. "Do not touch what is unclean, and I will receive you."

Col 3:2 Set your mind on things above, not on things on the earth.

* **2Tim 2:4** No one engaged in warfare entangles himself with the affairs of this life, that he may please him who enlisted him as a soldier.

Pr 1:10 My son, if sinners entice you, do not consent.

* **Mt 10:16** Behold, I send you out as sheep in the midst of wolves. Therefore be wise as serpents and harmless as doves.

Mt 10:25 It is enough for a disciple that he be like his teacher, and a servant like his master. If they have called the master of the house Beelzebub, how much more will they call those of his household!

Mk 4:11, 12 And He said to them, "To you it has been given to know the mystery of the kingdom of God; but to those who are outside, all things come in parables, so that seeing they may see and not perceive, and hearing they may hear and not understand; lest they should turn, and their sins be forgiven them.

Mk 6:4b-6 But Jesus said to them, "A prophet is not without honor except in his own country, among his own relatives, and in his own house." Now He could not do many mighty works there, except that He laid His hands on a few sick people and healed them. And He marveled because of their unbelief.

* **Mk 8:36-38** For what will it profit a man if he gains the whole world, and loses his own soul? Or what will a man give in exchange for his soul? For whoever is ashamed of Me and My words in this adulterous and sinful generation, of him the Son

VI. DISCIPLESHIP MEANS "WALKING OUT" YOUR FAITH

of Man also will be ashamed when He comes in the glory of His Father with the holy angels.

Jn 17:14-16 I have given them Your word; and the world has hated them because they are not of the world, just as I am not of the world. I do not pray that You should take them out of the world, but that You should keep them from the evil one. They are not of the world, just as I am not of the world.

Jn 17:17-19 Sanctify them by Your truth. Your word is truth. As You sent Me into the world, I also have sent them into the world. And for their sakes I sanctify Myself, that they also may be sanctified by the truth.

Ro 8:5 For those who live according to the flesh set their minds on the things of the flesh, but those who live according to the Spirit, the things of the Spirit.

* **Ro 12:2** Do not be conformed to this world, but be transformed by the renewing of your mind, that you may prove what is that good and acceptable and perfect will of God.

1Cor 2:14 But the natural man does not receive the things of the Spirit of God, for they are foolishness to him; nor can he know them, because they are spiritually discerned.

1Cor 10:21 You cannot drink the cup of the Lord and the cup of demons; you cannot partake of the Lord's table and of the table of demons.

1Jn 5:19 We know that we are of God, and the whole world lies under the sway of the wicked one.

2Cor 7:1 Therefore, having these promises, beloved, let us cleanse ourselves from all filthiness of the flesh and spirit, perfecting holiness in the fear of God.

* **1Jn 2:15** Do not love the world or the things in the world. If anyone loves the world, the love of the Father is not in him. For all that is in the world—the lust of the flesh, the lust of the eyes, and the pride of life—is not of the Father but is of the world.

And the world is passing away, and the lust of it; but he who does the will of God abides forever.

* **Jam 4:4** Adulterers and adulteresses! Do you not know that friendship with the world is enmity with God? Whoever therefore wants to be a friend of the world makes himself an enemy of God.

A Surrendered Life (Not My Will)

Surrender does not come naturally to most of us. It is difficult for the carnal mind to let go because we think we have all of the answers and can make all of the decisions. Surrendering our will to God and then seeking His will for us in our daily lives or for our future, requires great <u>trust</u> in His love for us. However, when we know how much God loves us, we <u>can</u> surrender to His care and guidance. God desires surrender, because it is a demonstration of our utter dependence and <u>trust</u> in Him. Surrendering to Him gives us a peace of mind and contentment of heart that surpasses understanding.

Jn 5:30b I do not seek My own will but the will of the Father who sent Me.

* **Pr 3:5, 6** Trust in the Lord with all your heart, And lean not on your own understanding; In all your ways acknowledge Him, and He shall direct your paths.

Ps 37:5 Commit your way to the Lord, trust also in Him, and He shall bring it to pass.

Jn 6:38 For I have come down from heaven, not to do My own will, but the will of Him who sent Me.

* **Ro 12:1, 2** I beseech you therefore, brethren, by the mercies of God, that you present your bodies a <u>living sacrifice</u>, holy, acceptable to God, which is your reasonable service. And do not be conformed to this world, but be transformed by the renewing of your mind, that you may prove what is that good and acceptable and perfect will of God.

VI. DISCIPLESHIP MEANS "WALKING OUT" YOUR FAITH

Ps 40:8 I delight to do Your will, O my God, and Your law is within my heart.

Ps 143:10 Teach me to do Your will, for You are my God; Your Spirit is good. Lead me in the land of uprightness.

* **Lk 22:42** Father, if it is Your will, take this cup away from Me; nevertheless <u>not My will</u>, but Yours be done.

* **Jn 3:30** He must increase, but I must decrease.

Jn 4:34 Jesus said to them, "My food is to do the will of Him who sent Me, and to finish His work."

* **Ro 6:13a** Do not present your members as instruments of unrighteousness to sin, but present yourselves to God.

1Pt 5:7 Casting all your care upon Him, for He cares for you.

* **Jam 4:7** Therefore submit to God. Resist the devil and he will flee from you.

Ps 27:11 Teach me Your way, O Lord, and lead me in a smooth path.

Raising Children is "Discipling"

Raising children is one of the greatest responsibilities ever given to man by God. As Christians, that responsibility is even more important due to our accountability in knowing the truth of His Word. God wants us to impact to them all the principles of His Word at an early age so that when they grow older, they will not depart from it. (See Pr 22:6)

Parents have the opportunity to mold the lives of their children into the living example of a child of God. It takes consistency, discipline, patience, endurance and virtually every other God-given gift to rise to the task. It is hard work to discipline (train) children to guide and mold them into what they should become in the Lord, but the fruits are eternally rewarding, knowing that our children are strong in the values, principles, truth and love of God.

Coaches win gold medals too. Parents and coaches are the truly rewarded. Except their medal doesn't hang around their neck; it's around their heart. They get to cherish all the potential they were believing in and paid a mighty price for. It's the countless hours of sacrificing and training that turn into wings of glory for the one(s) they've given everything to. But God made it so that there's a greater reward in giving than in receiving. *"It is more blessed to give than to receive" (Acts 20:35)*. And there is another law of God at work in parenting. *"Unless a grain of wheat falls into the ground and dies, it remains alone; but if it dies, it produces much grain" (Jn 12:24)*.

Parenting is the most challenging task in one's life, because it's a constant sacrifice and unending dying to oneself for the wellbeing of the children. But parents find their fulfilment, their joy and their life's greatest accomplishment in their children. Their fulfilment is in the happy visage of their kids. That's why training is "discipling". It's an act of forming and training a WINNER. You can't have a happy child without discipline. When the child has no boundaries, he's confused and unruly. While disciplining is a constant and a vigilant exercise, not disciplining a child can result in so much pain. The price of regret is always greater than the price of discipline. Parents must count the cost from the start.

3Jn 1:4 I have no greater joy than to hear that my children walk in truth.

Mt 18:5, 6, 10a Whoever receives one little child like this in My name receives Me. But whoever causes one of these little ones who believe in Me to sin, it would be better for him if a millstone were hung around his neck, and he were drowned in the depth of the sea. Take heed that you do not despise one of these little ones.

* **Ps 127:3-5a** Children are a heritage from the Lord. The fruit of the womb is a reward. Like arrows in the hand of a warrior, so are the children of one's youth. Happy is the man who has his quiver full of them.

Ps 144:12 That our sons may be as plants grown up in their youth; that our daughters may be as pillars, sculptured in palace style.

VI. DISCIPLESHIP MEANS "WALKING OUT" YOUR FAITH

Pr 17:6 Children's children are the crown of old men, and the glory of children is their father.

Pr 20:7 The righteous man walks in his integrity; his children are blessed after him.

* **Ecc 8:11** Because the sentence against an evil work is not executed speedily, therefore the heart of the sons of men is fully set in them to do evil.

Ps 34:11 Come, you children, listen to me; I will teach you the fear of the Lord.

Ps 119:9 How can a young man cleanse his way? By taking heed according to Your word.

Pr 3:12 For whom the Lord loves He corrects, just as a father the son in whom he delights.

Pr 8:32, 33 Now therefore, listen to me, my children, for blessed are those who keep my ways. Hear instruction and be wise, and do not disdain it.

Pr 13:1 A wise son heeds his father's instruction, but a scoffer does not listen to rebuke.

Pr 13:24 He who spares his rod hates his son, but he who loves him disciplines him promptly.

* **Pr 22:6** Train up a child in the way he should go, and when he is old he will not depart from it.

* **Pr 22:15** Foolishness is bound up in the heart of a child; the rod of correction will drive it far from him.

Pr 29:15 The rod and rebuke give wisdom, but a child left to himself brings shame to his mother.

* **Isa 54:13** All your children shall be taught by the Lord, and great shall be the peace of your children.

* **Jn 10:11b** The good shepherd gives His life for the sheep.

Eph 6:1-4 Children, obey your parents in the Lord, for this is right. Honor your father and mother, which is the first commandment with promise: That it may be well with you and you may live long on the earth. And you, fathers, do not provoke your children to wrath, but bring them up in the training and admonition of the Lord.

Heb 12:9-11 Furthermore, we have had human fathers who corrected us, and we paid them respect. Shall we not much more readily be in subjection to the Father of spirits and live? For they indeed for a few days chastened us as seemed best to them, but He for our profit, that we may be partakers of His holiness. Now no chastening seems to be joyful for the present, but painful; nevertheless, afterward it yields the peaceable fruit of righteousness to those who have been trained by it.

* **Heb 12:6, 11** For whom the Lord loves He chastens, and scourges every son whom He receives. Now no chastening seems to be joyful for the present, but painful; nevertheless, afterward it yields the peaceable fruit of righteousness to those who have been trained by it.

* **Pr 15:32** He who disdains instruction despises his own soul, but he who heeds rebuke gets understanding.

Pr 16:6 In mercy and truth atonement is provided for iniquity; and by the fear of the Lord one departs from evil.

Col 3:20 Children, obey your parents in all things, for this is well pleasing to the Lord.

1Tim 4:12 Let no one despise your youth, but be an example to the believers in word, in conduct, in love, in spirit, in faith, in purity.

VII. WINNING THE SPIRITUAL WARFARE

Once you are born again, you have joined the winning side! Jesus has triumphed over every principality (Col 2:15). He is the name above of all names. This is why a Christian must walk in victory, not <u>towards</u> a victory but <u>from</u> the victory that Christ has already won. Winning the spiritual warfare has everything to do with knowing <u>who we are in Christ</u>. Not only has He won the victory, but He made sure we would have the power and the authority to win every victory, and to destroy the works of the devil as He did. We are fully equipped to win, but we must <u>use our weapons</u> to keep defeating the enemy. The Bible compares us to warriors. Soldiers have to be willing to give up their freedom in order to preserve others' freedom. Sacrificing is part of developing our character as disciples. The Apostle Paul said, *"Endure hardship as a good soldier of Jesus Christ" (2Tim 2:3)*.

The Christian life is warfare; an intense conflict waged against intense foes ever seeking to entrap, deceive and ruin the souls of men. It demands the putting forth of full and constant spiritual energy against invisible foes, in order to remain 'more than a conqueror'. (See Ro 8:37). An active Christian must endure hardness as a good soldier. It's part and parcel for winning; it demands constant vigilance. We wrestle against wicked spirits in high places. (See Eph 6:12). Discipline, self-denial, hardship and determination all belong to the military lifestyle of Christianity. We are called to destroy the works of Satan, not to just co-exist with them. Eternal vigilance is the price of victory. *"Do not let the sun go down on your wrath" (Eph 4:26). "Watching therefore with all perseverance and supplication" (Eph 6:18).* You don't lose til you quit. Most people lose their miracle just before it comes. The enemy cannot win until you quit.

The War is in the Mind~Renewing the Mind

The enemy's war against us first takes place in our mind and emotions. Even though saved and born again, there is a fight between our spiritual birthright and our physical birthright. The devil knows that nothing can be done about our spirit since it already belongs to and is dedicated to Christ. And since the devil is the father of lies (Jn 8:44), he uses our minds to control our thoughts and actions. His goal is to get your mind off of the promises of God through those mental attacks. But in our 'new man', we have the 'mind of Christ' (1 Cor 2:15). With the Word of God, we can go to war against the enemy's attacks on our mind and learn to replace the lies with the truths of God. Our human mind was not created to think evil thoughts. When you think evil in anger, bitterness, unforgiveness, etc., your mind cannot process these thoughts properly and you end up destroying what you're trying to build. The apostle Paul said, *"Whatsoever things are true, whatsoever things are honest, whatsoever things are just, whatsoever things are of good report, if there be any virtue, if there be any praise, think on these things" (Phil 4:8).*

Actually, Satan cannot do anything to you without your consent. He can only use your power of choice; and he does so by mixing a little bit of truth to get your attention and floods you with lies. That's why it's important to get filled up with the Word so you can discern the attacks on your mind. Paul said, *"Neither give place to the devil" (Eph 4:27).* The battle is between our old nature and our 'new nature'. It's a daily conflict between God's plan for us and our own plan. It's a battle against our ego, really, and it requires discipline of our thoughts. One of Satan's favorite devices is compromise, to choose the easier way. He makes comfort and complacency appealing. Most of our habits are centered on these two, but complacency is the enemy of victory.

That's why we have to reevaluate our wrong habits, whether they be physical or emotional. No one likes the pain of discipline, but it will bear lasting fruits in your life. It's a battle between short-term gratification and long-term benefit. Satan plays with our emotions and tries to make us live out those emotions in the

VII. WINNING THE SPIRITUAL WARFARE

carnal for immediate gratification. But God gives us the power to rearrange our own life.

We must first win the battle in our own mind. We must be willing to discipline ourselves to be more Christ-like. Romans 12:1, 2 says, *"I beseech you therefore brethren by the mercies of God that you present your body a living sacrifice, wholly, acceptable unto God and <u>do not</u> be conformed to this world, but be transformed by the <u>renewing</u> of your mind, that you may prove what is that good and acceptable and perfect will of God"*.

In other words, do not let this world conform you or mold you so that you look, talk and live like the world. But rather, let what is in you be seen on the outside. It's only by your mind being renewed by the Word of God that you truly change your character. Your mind is renewed to the degree that the Word of God dictates your behavior.

Renewing your mind doesn't mean thinking on the things of God just the five first minutes of your day during your devotional time; but your whole character, your whole day, is dictated by your new man. It is in knowing God's Word that the Spirit of God in you comes through your body, your emotions, and your intentions. You act out Jesus. Your thinking becomes more like Christ's. Your whole self becomes effaced, denied, and the love of Christ living in you, loves on people unselfishly. That's what renewing our mind is about. It is the effort of disciplining our thoughts to fall in line with the principles and the laws of God.

* **Ro 12:1, 2** I beseech you therefore, brethren, by the mercies of God, that you present your bodies a living sacrifice, holy, acceptable to God, which is your reasonable service. And do not be <u>conformed</u> to this world, but be <u>transformed</u> by the renewing of your mind, that you may prove what is that good and acceptable and perfect will of God.

* **1Tim 6:12** Fight the good fight of faith, lay hold on eternal life, whereunto thou art also called, and hast professed a good profession before many witnesses.

1Cor 2:14, 16 But the natural man does not receive the things of the Spirit of God, for they are foolishness to him; nor can he know them, because they are spiritually discerned. For who has known the mind of the Lord that he may instruct Him? But we have the mind of Christ.

Phil 2:5 Let this mind be in you which was also in Christ Jesus.

2Cor 11:3 But I fear, lest somehow, as the serpent deceived Eve by his craftiness, so your minds may be corrupted from the simplicity that is in Christ.

Jam 4:4 Adulterers and adulteresses! Do you not know that friendship with the world is enmity with God? Whoever therefore wants to be a friend of the world makes himself an enemy of God.

1Pt 1:13 Therefore gird up the loins of your mind, be sober, and rest your hope fully upon the grace that is to be brought to you at the revelation of Jesus Christ.

Pr 4:23 Keep your heart with all diligence, for out of it spring the issues of life.

Col 3:2 Set your mind on things above, not on things on the earth.

1Pt 5:8 Be sober, be vigilant; because your adversary the devil walks about like a roaring lion, seeking whom he may devour.

Ro 8:13 For if you live according to the flesh you will die; but if by the Spirit you put to death the deeds of the body, you will live.

* **2Tim 1:7** For God has not given us a spirit of fear, but of power and of love and of a sound mind.

Eph 6:12 For we do not wrestle against flesh and blood, but against principalities, against powers, against the rulers of the darkness of this age, against spiritual hosts of wickedness in the heavenly places.

Ro 12:1, 2 I beseech you therefore, brethren, by the mercies of God, that you present your bodies a living sacrifice, holy, acceptable to God, which is your reasonable service. And do not be conformed to this world, but be transformed by the

VII. WINNING THE SPIRITUAL WARFARE

renewing of your mind, that you may prove what is that good and acceptable and perfect will of God.

Ro 8:5-7 For those who live according to the flesh set their minds on the things of the flesh, but those who live according to the Spirit, the things of the Spirit. For to be carnally minded is death, but to be spiritually minded is life and peace. Because the carnal mind is enmity against God; for it is not subject to the law of God, nor indeed can be.

Gal 5:17 For the flesh lusts against the Spirit, and the Spirit against the flesh; and these are contrary to one another, so that you do not do the things that you wish.

Ro 7:23 But I see another law in my members, warring against the law of my mind, and bringing me into captivity to the law of sin which is in my members.

1Pt 1:13 Therefore gird up the loins of your mind, be sober, and rest your hope fully upon the grace that is to be brought to you at the revelation of Jesus Christ.

Pr 23:7 For as he thinks in his heart, so is he.

* **Isa 26:3** You will keep him in perfect peace, whose mind is stayed on You, because he trusts in You.

* **Isa 59:19b** When the Enemy shall come in like a flood, the Spirit of the Lord shall lift up a standard against him.

* **2Cor 10:3-5** For though we walk in the flesh, we do not war according to the flesh. For the weapons of our warfare are not carnal but mighty in God for pulling down strongholds, casting down arguments and every high thing that exalts itself against the knowledge of God, bringing every thought into captivity to
* the obedience of Christ.

* **Mt 4:10** Then Jesus said to him, "Away with you, Satan! For it is written, 'You shall worship the Lord your God, and Him only you shall serve.'"

Ro 8:5-7 For those who live according to the flesh set their minds on the things of the flesh, but those who live according to the Spirit, the things of the Spirit. For to be carnally minded is death, but to be spiritually minded is life and peace. Because the carnal mind is enmity against God; for it is not subject to the law of God, nor indeed can be.

Ps 1:1, 2 Blessed is the man who walks not in the counsel of the ungodly, nor stands in the path of sinners, nor sits in the seat of the scornful; but his delight is in the law of the Lord, and in His law he meditates day and night.

* **Phil 4:8** Finally, brethren, whatever things are true, whatever things are noble, whatever things are just, whatever things are pure, whatever things are lovely, whatever things are of good report, if there is any virtue and if there is anything praiseworthy—meditate on these things.

2Tim 2:22 Flee also youthful lusts; but pursue righteousness, faith, love, peace with those who call on the Lord out of a pure heart.

Pr 4:20-23 My son, give attention to my words; incline your ear to my sayings. Do not let them depart from your eyes; keep them in the midst of your heart; for they are life to those who find them, and health to all their flesh. Keep your heart with all diligence, for out of it spring the issues of life.

Ps 19:7 The law of the Lord is perfect, converting the soul; the testimony of the Lord is sure, making wise the simple.

* **Heb 4:12** For the word of God is living and powerful, and sharper than any two-edged sword, piercing even to the division of soul and spirit, and of joints and marrow, and is a discerner of the thoughts and intents of the heart.

How to be "More than Conquerors"

The authority of Christ has been given to every believer. It is important to appropriate the power and dominion which has been embedded in our new identity and inheritance. The way to be more than a conqueror, is to <u>exercise</u> and <u>make use</u> of the weapons of warfare that God has given us.

VII. WINNING THE SPIRITUAL WARFARE

* **1Tim 6:12** Fight the good fight of faith, lay hold on eternal life, to which you were also called and have confessed the good confession in the presence of many witnesses.
* **1Jn 3:8b** For this purpose the Son of God was manifested, that He might destroy the works of the devil.

  1Jn 5:5 Who is he who overcomes the world, but he who believes that Jesus is the Son of God?

* **1Jn 4:4** You are of God, little children, and have overcome them, because He who is in you is greater than he who is in the world.

  Jn 14:12 He who believes in Me, the works that I do he will do also; and greater works than these he will do, because I go to My Father.

  Lk 10:17 Then the seventy returned with joy, saying, "Lord, even the demons are subject to us in Your name".

  Mt 16:19 And I will give you the keys of the kingdom of heaven, and whatever you bind on earth will be bound in heaven, and whatever you loose on earth will be loosed in heaven.

  Phil 2:9-11 Therefore God also has highly exalted Him and given Him the name which is above every name, that at the name of Jesus every knee should bow, of those in heaven, and of those on earth, and of those under the earth, and that every tongue should confess that Jesus Christ is Lord, to the glory of God the Father.

* **Isa 59:19b** When the enemy comes in like a flood, the Spirit of the Lord will lift up a standard against him.
* **Jam 4:7** Therefore submit to God. Resist the devil and he will flee from you.

  Ro 8:35-37 Who shall separate us from the love of Christ? Shall tribulation, or distress, or persecution, or famine, or nakedness, or peril, or sword? As it is written: "For Your sake we are killed all day long; We are accounted as sheep for the slaughter." Yet in all these things we are more than conquerors through Him who loved us.

Phil 3:8 Yet indeed I also count all things loss for the excellence of the knowledge of Christ Jesus my Lord, for whom I have suffered the loss of all things, and count them as rubbish, that I may gain Christ.

Col 1:12-13 Giving thanks to the Father who has qualified us to be partakers of the inheritance of the saints in the light. He has delivered us from the power of darkness and conveyed us into the kingdom of the Son of His love.

* **1Jn 2:14b** The word of God abides in you, and you have overcome the wicked one.

    Rev 3:5 He who overcomes shall be clothed in white garments, and I will not blot out his name from the book of life; but I will confess his name before My Father and before His angels.

* **Eph 4:27** Nor give place to the devil.
* **2Cor 10:4, 5** For the weapons of our warfare are not carnal but mighty in God for pulling down strongholds, casting down arguments and every high thing that exalts itself against the knowledge of God, bringing every thought into captivity to the obedience of Christ,
* **Eph 6:16** Above all, taking the shield of faith with which you will be able to quench all the fiery darts of the wicked one.
* **2Tim 4:18** And the Lord will deliver me from every evil work and preserve me for His heavenly kingdom. To Him be glory forever and ever. Amen!

Be "On Guard"

For as long as we live in this world (the kingdom of darkness), the prince of this world will continue to attack and distract us from accomplishing what God has purposed for us. This is why we must constantly be aware of the devices of the devil and be "on guard", as a warrior should be! It takes consistent discipline to guard our mind, emotions and actions against the tricks and the devices of Satan, but that's what resisting the enemy and being sober and vigilant is about. And the best tool to resist

VII. WINNING THE SPIRITUAL WARFARE

him with is quoting the Word of God. That's how Jesus resisted Satan in the wilderness (Lk 4:1-13).

2Cor 2:11 Lest Satan should take advantage of us; for we are not ignorant of his devices.

1Pt 5:8 Be sober, be vigilant for your adversary the devil walks about as a roaring lion, seeking whom he may devour.

* **Mt 26:41** Watch and pray, lest you enter into temptation. The spirit indeed is willing, but the flesh is weak.

* **Lk 22:31b, 32** Simon! Indeed, Satan has asked for you, that he may sift you as wheat. But I have prayed for you, that your faith should not fail; and when you have returned to Me, strengthen your brethren.

Ro 13:14 But put on the Lord Jesus Christ, and make no provision for the flesh, to fulfill its lusts.

* **1Cor 10:13** No temptation has overtaken you except such as is common to man; but God is faithful, who will not allow you to be tempted beyond what you are able, but with the temptation will also make the way of escape, that you may be able to bear it.

* **Eph 6:10-12** Finally, my brethren, be strong in the Lord and in the power of His might. Put on the whole armor of God, that you may be able to stand against the wiles of the devil. For we do not wrestle against flesh and blood, but against principalities, against powers, against the rulers of the darkness of this age, against spiritual hosts of wickedness in the heavenly places.

Eph 6:14, 16, 17 Stand therefore, having girded your waist with truth, having put on the breastplate of righteousness. Above all, taking the shield of faith with which you will be able to quench all the fiery darts of the wicked one. And take the helmet of salvation, and the sword of the Spirit, which is the word of God.

1Thes 5:5-8 You are all sons of light and sons of the day. We are not of the night nor of darkness. Therefore let us not sleep, as others do, but let us watch and be sober. For those who sleep, sleep at night, and those who get drunk are drunk at night. But let us who are of the day be sober, putting on the breastplate of faith and love, and as a helmet the hope of salvation.

* **Heb 12:1, 2** Therefore we also, since we are surrounded by so great a cloud of witnesses, let us lay aside every weight, and the sin which so easily ensnares us, and let us run with endurance the race that is set before us, looking unto Jesus, the author and finisher of our faith, who for the joy that was set before Him endured the cross, despising the shame, and has sat down at the right hand of the throne of God.

* **1Pt 4:12, 13** Beloved, do not think it strange concerning the fiery trial which is to try you, as though some strange thing happened to you; but rejoice to the extent that you partake of Christ's sufferings, that when His glory is revealed, you may also be glad with exceeding joy.

* **1Pt 5:8, 9a** Be sober, be vigilant; because your adversary the devil walks about like a roaring lion, seeking whom he may devour. Resist him, steadfast in the faith.

* **Isa 43:1b, 2** Fear not, for I have redeemed you; I have called you by your name; you are Mine. When you pass through the waters, I will be with you; and through the rivers, they shall not overflow you. When you walk through the fire, you shall not be burned, nor shall the flame scorch you.

* **Ro 8:18** For I consider that the sufferings of this present time are not worthy to be compared with the glory which shall be revealed in us.

* **Jam 1:12** Blessed is the man who endures temptation; for when he has been approved, he will receive the crown of life which the Lord has promised to those who love Him.

* **Jn 15:2** Every branch in Me that does not bear fruit He takes away; and every branch that bears fruit He prunes, that it may bear more fruit.

* **Ps 119:67** Before I was afflicted I went astray, But now I keep Your word.

VII. WINNING THE SPIRITUAL WARFARE

* **Ps 119:71** It is good for me that I have been afflicted, that I may learn Your statutes.
* **Jam 1:2, 3** My brethren, count it all joy when you fall into various trials, knowing that the testing of your faith produces patience.
* **Heb 5:8** Though He was a Son, yet He learned obedience by the things which He suffered.
* **1Pt 1:7** That the genuineness of your faith, being much more precious than gold that perishes, though it is tested by fire, may be found to praise, honor, and glory at the revelation of Jesus Christ,
* **2Tim 2:3** You therefore must endure hardship as a good soldier of Jesus Christ.

VIII. FREELY YOU HAVE RECEIVED, FREELY GIVE

Jesus commissioned His disciples to preach the gospel, heal the sick, to cast out demons, to cleanse the lepers, to raise the dead, and to basically destroy all the works of the devil, just as He did. (See Mt 10:8) *"Jesus went about everywhere healing all manner of sickness and disease" (Mt 4:23, 24)*. Now, we, as His disciples, have the same commission and the same power as the early disciples and as Jesus Himself.

Discipleship 101 is: *"The works that I (Jesus) do he will do also" (Jn 14:12)*. We heal in His name and in His stead. We use His authority and His victory. We are appointed ministers of the gospel of Jesus Christ. That basically means that we've been deputized as officers enforcing the kingdom of God on earth. We know what God's Word says and we enforce it and we never back off from it. We don't waver and we don't quit till the devil lets up. That's one time when stubbornness is a quality. Don't fear repeating yourself with God's Word. It carries the necessary authority. We shouldn't ever get used to losing. We believe relentlessly.

Also, remember, it's our responsibility to meet the need. –Jesus did. He said, *"Give to any man that asks you" (Lk 6:30)*. You can have faith for people who don't have faith. It's the Christian's job to help. (Re-read the parable of the good Samaritan in Luke 10:25-37). We must see their need as our need. Once we have received the baptism, we have everything we need to meet the need. The secret of our success in the great commission is in the Holy Ghost power. You don't need anything else to add to it.

Jesus did not ask us to pray for the sick. He said, "Heal the sick" *(Mt 10:8)*. It's a command from Him to command the devil off its prey. We are to command healing. It's okay to be aggressive and militant about it, and speak with authority to destroy the works of the devil. (See Mat 9:29) We don't beg God to do it.. He gave us the authority to heal. We are to lay hands on the sick and heal them. He gave us His name to use at will. We have the ability and the responsibility to fix what's wrong. We can't fail if we don't give up. Love never fails and love never quits.

The only reason we would fail is if we either do not believe the Word or are bound to the traditions of man and the doctrines of religion such as:

- ~ Sickness will make you a <u>better</u> person.
- ~ God is dealing with you; He may not be done with you.
- ~ God needed another flower in His garden in heaven.
- ~ It's because of generational curses.
- ~ You don't have enough faith.
- ~ Healing was for the apostles.
- ~ I don't have <u>that</u> gift.
- ~ It's not <u>always</u> God's will to heal.
- ~ It doesn't work <u>every</u> time.
- ~ The person you prayed for didn't have the faith.
- ~ Sickness is caused by sin.
- ~ What did that person <u>do</u> to deserve that?

Let's refuse to believe lies, and insist and persist in faith. We're not the ones doing the healing; God is. Signs follow believers, not just pastors or the original apostles. Do not be discouraged if you don't see the results right away. The Word works because it is based on God's unwavering faithfulness to keep His Word. Just because you don't see it, doesn't mean it is not working. Farmers plant seed all day and after it's planted, they can't see the plant, but it's growing and the crops will follow. It's the same for believers. The more you start laying hands, the more you will see results because the more the devil will see you mean business. Faith is simply not giving up believing.

Jesus Healed ALL that were Sick

Jesus healed everyone, all who were sick and oppressed. There are no examples where Jesus did not heal the sick because of generational curses, or because God still had lessons to teach them, or if they were too big a sinner or they were a Jew or

Gentile, or if they needed to stay sick a little longer to work out their righteousness! None of that. Jesus' example was one of willingness, mercy and compassion to heal! *"When the sun was setting, all those who had any that were sick with various diseases brought them to Him; and He laid His hands on every one of them and healed them" (Lk 4:40).*

Mt 4:23, 24 And Jesus went about all Galilee, teaching in their synagogues, preaching the gospel of the kingdom, and healing all kinds of sickness and all kinds of disease among the people. Then His fame went throughout all Syria; and they brought to Him all sick people who were afflicted with various diseases and torments, and those who were demon-possessed, epileptics, and paralytics; and He healed them.

Mt 8:16, 17 When evening had come, they brought to Him many who were demon-possessed. And He cast out the spirits with a word, and healed all who were sick, that it might be fulfilled which was spoken by Isaiah the prophet, saying: "He Himself took our infirmities and bore our sicknesses."

Mt 14:14 And when Jesus went out He saw a great multitude; and He was moved with compassion for them, and healed their sick.

Lk 4:39 So He stood over her and rebuked the fever, and it left her. And immediately she arose and served them.

Lk 4:40 When the sun was setting, all those who had any that were sick with various diseases brought them to Him; and He laid His hands on every one of them and healed them.

Lk 9:11 But when the multitudes knew it, they followed Him; and He received them and spoke to them about the kingdom of God, and healed those who had need of healing.

Acts 10:38 How God anointed Jesus of Nazareth with the Holy Spirit and with power, who went about doing good and healing all who were oppressed by the devil, for God was with Him.

Authority to Heal the Sick, Cast out Demons, Raise the Dead, Cleanse the Lepers

Once you are born again, you are empowered with Jesus living in you and working through you. And because of His great love and compassion for people, He wants to heal all that are sick, set the captives free, deliver the oppressed and show the manifestation of God's kingdom on earth now, as it is in heaven. And this is the authority and the power that He has invested in all believers. Jesus has delivered us from all the "can't do", "can't be', "can't have". We have light power over darkness. But God is waiting on man to command things into existence.

We're commanded by the Lord to lay hands on the sick. *"They shall lay hands on the sick and they shall recover" (Mk 16:18b)*. We do not lay hands on the sick because we see them recover, but because we obey Jesus' command. So, do not focus on the victories or failures, but on loving God and loving your neighbor. Determine to continue laying hands on the sick regardless of what you see take place. The results will come as you persevere. The devil will try you when you don't see results right away, but you won't let up if you mean business.

Remember that Jesus did not say to pray for the sick. He said to heal the sick. It is a command that He gave to us. And He would not have given us this command without the authority to be able to do it. So, whenever you lay hands on someone, and command healing, ask them to check if they're healed. If not, pray again! And pray again, until you outlast the devil. Remember, all sicknesses are works of the devil and Jesus came for this purpose, "to destroy the works of the devil". (See 1Jn 3:8)

* **Mt 10:1** And when He had called His twelve disciples to Him, He gave them power over unclean spirits, to cast them out, and to heal all kinds of sickness and all kinds of disease.

Mt 10:7, 8 And as you go, preach, saying, 'The kingdom of heaven is at hand.' Heal the sick, cleanse the lepers, and raise the dead, cast out demons. Freely you have received, freely give.

* Mk 16:17, 18 These signs will follow those who believe: in My name they will cast out demons; they will speak with new tongues; they will take up serpents; and if they drink anything deadly, it will by no means hurt them; they will lay hands on the sick, and they will recover.

Lk 9:1, 2 Then He called His twelve disciples together and gave them power and authority over all demons, and to cure diseases. He sent them to preach the kingdom of God and to heal the sick.

Lk 10:19 I give you the authority to trample on serpents and scorpions, and over all the power of the enemy, and nothing shall by any means hurt you.

Jn 14:12-14 Most assuredly, I say to you, he who believes in Me, the works that I do he will do also; and greater works than these he will do, because I go to My Father. And whatever you ask in My name, that I will do, that the Father may be glorified in the Son. If you ask anything in My name, I will do it.

YOU can be Healed Too!

God's will is for us to be whole in body, mind and spirit. (See 1Thes 5:23) We must not accept sickness, but rather rebuke it as one of the lies and oppressions of the devil. Use your voice with God's Word (His supernatural medicine) to resist sickness that comes against you. Sickness is never the final word. God's Word is the final word! Use His promises of healing to speak to your body so that it obeys and falls in line with God's Word. The Bible says, *"He sent His Word and healed them, and delivered them from their destructions" (Ps 107:20).*

Rom 4:17 says, *"We call those things which be not as though they were"*. But calling those things that are, as though they're not is not faith. If you're sick, and you say, "I'm not sick", you're simply denying the fact. That's calling things that are as though they're not. We are to call those things that are not (yet) as though they are and they become. "By His stripes I'm healed. I'm taking the truth of His Word over what I feel. The fact is, I'm sick, but the truth is above the facts". You're agreeing with

VIII. FREELY YOU HAVE RECEIVED, FREELY GIVE

the truth. You're calling things that are not (yet) as though they were and they become manifested. You stand on His Word as though it were done, and it becomes so. You're focusing your faith on God's Word and you're agreeing with His truth to be manifested in you.

Mk 11:23 For assuredly, I say to you, "Whoever says to this mountain, 'Be removed and be cast into the sea,' and does not doubt in his heart, but believes that those things he says will be done, he will have whatever he says.'".

Eph 3:20 Now to Him who is able to do exceedingly abundantly above all that we ask or think, according to the power that works in us.

1Pt 2:24 Who Himself bore our sins in His own body on the tree, that we, having died to sins, might live for righteousness—by whose stripes you were healed.

* **Ps 107:20** He sent His Word and healed them, And delivered them from their destructions.

* **Jam 5:14, 15** Is anyone among you sick? Let him call for the elders of the church, and let them pray over him, anointing him with oil in the name of the Lord. And the prayer of faith shall save the sick, and the Lord shall raise him up.

3Jn 1:2 Beloved, I pray that you may prosper in all things and be in health, just as your soul prospers.

* **Jer 30:17a** "For I will restore health to you and heal you of your wounds," says the Lord.

* **Isa 53:5** He was wounded for our transgressions, He was bruised for our iniquities; The chastisement for our peace was upon Him, and by His stripes we are healed.

* **Mal 4:2a** But to you who fear My name the Son of righteousness shall arise with healing in His wings.

* **Ps 34:19** Many are the afflictions of the righteous, but the Lord delivers him out of them all.

* **Ps 103:3** Who forgives all your iniquities, who heals all your diseases.
* **Ps 147:3** He heals the brokenhearted and binds up their wounds.

    Pr 17:22 A merry heart does good, like medicine.
* **Isa 40:29** He gives power to the weak, and to those who have no might He increases strength.
* **Acts 9:34a** Jesus the Christ heals you.
* **Lk 17:14b** And so it was that as they went, they were cleansed.
* **2Kg 20:5b** I have heard your prayer, I have seen your tears; surely I will heal you.
* **Exo 15:26** If you diligently heed the voice of the Lord your God and do what is right in His sight, give ear to His commandments and keep all His statutes, I will put none of the diseases on you which I have brought on the Egyptians. For I am the Lord who heals you.
* **1Jn 1:9** If we confess our sins, He is faithful and just to forgive us our sins and to cleanse us from all unrighteousness.

IX. RELIGIOSITY VS CHRISTIANITY

The only times that Jesus was angry, in fact furious, is when He addressed the religious Pharisees (Mt 23:13-28). He exposed their hypocrisy, their self-righteous adherence to the letter of the law, while omitting mercy and love. He exposed how far they were from the righteousness of God by only reading and talking about the Word of God, and not <u>doing</u> it. Religious doctrines have done so much to divide the body of Christ and bring in rules and regulations that are simply not biblically scriptural and thereby lead God's people away from <u>obeying</u> the Word of God. Jesus said that the doctrines and traditions of man take out the life of God's powerful Word. The Word of God doesn't work simply by hearing it or hearing about it; it works if you work it by fully basing your faith in it and <u>working</u> your faith according to what it says. *"Faith without works is dead" (Jam 2; 20)*. Jesus insisted over and over on <u>not only hearing</u> but <u>doing</u> what His Word commands.

Mt 15:3 He answered and said to them, "Why do you also transgress the commandment of God because of your tradition?"

Mt 23:2, 3, 5a The Scribes and the Pharisees sit in Moses' seat. Therefore, whatever they tell you to observe, that observe and do, but do not do according to their works; for they say, and do not do. But all their works they do to be seen by men.

Mt 23:25 Woe to you, Scribes and Pharisees, hypocrites! For you cleanse the outside of the cup and dish, but inside they are full of extortion and self-indulgence.

Mk 7:13 Making the Word of God of no effect through your tradition which you have handed down. And many such things you do.

Mt 15:8 These people draw near to Me with their mouth, and honor Me with their lips, but their heart is far from Me.

Jer 3:15 And I will give you shepherds according to My heart, who will feed you with knowledge and understanding.

Hos 4:6a My people are destroyed for lack of knowledge.

Jam 1:22 But be doers of the word, and not hearers only, deceiving yourselves.

Mt 7:21-23 Not everyone who says to Me, 'Lord, Lord,' shall enter the kingdom of heaven, but he who does the will of My Father in heaven. Many will say to Me in that day, 'Lord, Lord, have we not prophesied in Your name, cast out demons in Your name, and done many wonders in Your name?' And then I will declare to them, 'I never knew you; depart from Me, you who <u>practice lawlessness</u>!'

Mt 15:14 Let them alone. They are blind leaders of the blind. And if the blind leads the blind, both will fall into a ditch.

Mt 23:11-13 But he who is greatest among you shall be your servant. And whoever exalts himself will be humbled, and he who humbles himself will be exalted. But woe to you, Scribes and Pharisees, hypocrites! For you shut up the kingdom of heaven against men; for you neither go in yourselves, nor do you allow those who are entering to go in.

Mk 8:38 Whoever is ashamed of Me and My words in this adulterous and sinful generation, of him the Son of Man also will be ashamed when He comes in the glory of His Father with the holy angels.

Mk 10:45 For even the Son of Man did not come to be served, but to serve, and to give His life a ransom for many.

Lk 15:4 What man of you, having a hundred sheep, if he loses one of them, does not leave the ninety-nine in the wilderness, and go after the one which is lost until he finds it?

Lk 18:11, 12 The Pharisee stood and prayed thus with himself, 'God, I thank You that I am not like other men: extortioners, unjust, adulterers, or even as this tax collector. I fast twice a week; I give tithes of all that I possess.'

IX. RELIGIOSITY VS CHRISTIANITY

Jn 4:23, 24 But the hour is coming, and now is, when the true worshipers will worship the Father in Spirit and truth; for the Father is seeking such to worship Him. God is Spirit, and those who worship Him must worship in Spirit and truth.

Jn 9:40, 41 Then some of the Pharisees who were with Him heard these words, and said to Him, "Are we blind also?" Jesus said to them, "If you were blind, you would have no sin; but now you say, 'we see' therefore your sin remains."

Jn 10:11 I am the good shepherd. The good shepherd gives His life for the sheep.

* **Acts 7:48** However, the Most High does not dwell in temples made with hands, as the prophet says.

1Cor 1:17 For Christ did not send me to baptize, but to preach the gospel, not with wisdom of words, lest the cross of Christ should be made of no effect.

1Cor 2:4 And my speech and my preaching were not with persuasive words of human wisdom, but in demonstration of the Spirit and of power.

Gal 1:6, 7 I marvel that you are turning away so soon from Him who called you in the grace of Christ, to a different gospel, which is not another; but there are some who trouble you and want to pervert the gospel of Christ.

Gal 1:9 As we have said before, so now I say again, if anyone preaches any other gospel to you than what you have received, let him be accursed.

Phil 4:9 The things which you learned and received and heard and saw in me, these do, and the God of peace will be with you.

* **1Tim 4:12** Let no one despise your youth, but be an example to the believers in word, in conduct, in love, in spirit, in faith, in purity.

1Pt 5:2, 3 Shepherd the flock of God which is among you, serving as overseers, not by compulsion but willingly, not for dishonest gain but eagerly; nor as being lords over those entrusted to you, but being examples to the flock.

1Jn 3:16 By this we know love, because He laid down His life for us. and we also ought to lay down our lives for the brethren.

The "Sacred Cows" of Religion

The "sacred cows" are the excuses and compromises that religion has tagged onto either God's words or the doing of the Word, and thereby robbing it of its power and effect. They quench the Spirit of God!

No one in history manifested more love than Jesus. He had compassion everywhere He went, whether for the sick, the oppressed, the hungry, the social outcast, the sinners, the captives, even the demonized. One man's soul was worth more to Him than the price of a whole herd of swine. But on the other hand, He burnt with anger against the religious, judgmental attitudes that led people to hell with practices, doctrines and traditions and commercialization. (See Mt 21:13)

Jesus exposed their hypocrisy, and their self-righteousness and He warned people not to follow what they do. Jesus said, *"Beware of the leaven of the Pharisees and of the leaven of Herod" (Mat 8:15)*. The leaven of Herod is 'political correctness'. The war is against the blinded eyes of man and what frees us is the truth. *"And you shall know the truth and the truth shall make you free" (Jn 8:32)*. The truth is what refutes lies. That is why it is so important for Christians to know the Word. The previous verse says, *"If you abide in My Word, then are you My disciples indeed...."* We are to live in His Word and live it out, both!

Mk 8:15 And He charged them, saying, "Take heed, beware of the leaven of the Pharisees and the leaven of Herod."

Mt 15:1-3 Then the Scribes and Pharisees who were from Jerusalem came to Jesus, saying, "Why do Your disciples transgress the tradition of the elders? For they do not wash their hands when they eat bread." He answered and said to them,

"Why do you also transgress the commandment of God because of your tradition?"

Jn 8:6 This they said, testing Him, that they might have something of which to accuse Him. But Jesus stooped down and wrote on the ground with His finger, as though He did not hear.

Mt 15:12 Then His disciples came and said to Him, "Do You know that the Pharisees were offended when they heard this saying?"

Mt 19:3 The Pharisees also came to Him, testing Him, and saying to Him, "Is it lawful for a man to divorce his wife for just any reason?"

Lk 5:30 And the Scribes and the Pharisees complained against His disciples, saying, "Why do You eat and drink with tax collectors and sinners?"

Lk 6:7 So the Scribes and Pharisees watched Him closely, whether He would heal on the Sabbath, that they might find an accusation against Him.

Lk 11:39 Then the Lord said to him, "Now you Pharisees make the outside of the cup and dish clean, but your inward part is full of greed and wickedness".

Lk 11:53, 54 And as He said these things to them, the Scribes and the Pharisees began to assail Him vehemently, and to cross-examine Him about many things, lying in wait for Him, and seeking to catch Him in something He might say, that they might accuse Him.

Lk 16:14 Now the Pharisees, who were lovers of money, also heard all these things, and they derided Him.

Jn 7:32 The Pharisees heard the crowd murmuring these things concerning Him, and the Pharisees and the chief priests sent officers to take Him.

Jn 11:47 Then the chief priests and the Pharisees gathered a council and said, "What shall we do? For this Man works many signs."

Mt 15:6b-9 Jesus said, "Thus you have made the commandment of God of no effect by your tradition. Hypocrites! Well did Isaiah prophesy about you, saying: 'These people draw near to Me with their mouth, and honor Me with their lips, but their heart is far from Me'. But in vain they do worship me, teaching for doctrines the commandments of men."

1Tim 4:1-5 Now the Spirit expressly says that in latter times some will depart from the faith, giving heed to deceiving spirits and doctrines of demons, speaking lies in hypocrisy, having their own conscience seared with a hot iron, forbidding to marry, and commanding to abstain from foods which God created to be received with thanksgiving by those who believe and know the truth. For every creature of God is good, and nothing is to be refused if it is received with thanksgiving; for it is sanctified by the Word of God and prayer.

Beware of Self-Righteousness

When we are self-righteous, we act like we know more than others, and we are often stuck on the letter-of-the-law rather than being guided by love. Our judgments of others are then critical and condemning. God's righteousness so far exceeds our own! God says that our righteousness is in Him only. (See Ro 10:3) We cannot mix the goodness of God with our own goodness. God has paid the full price for our righteousness. This is why we must walk in meekness and humility. God resists the proud but gives grace unto the humble.

Lk 18:9-14 Also He spoke this parable to some who trusted in themselves that they were righteous, and despised others: Two men went up to the temple to pray, one a Pharisee and the other a tax collector. The Pharisee stood and prayed thus with himself, "God, I thank You that I am not like other men—extortionists, unjust, adulterers, or even as this tax collector. I fast twice a week; I give tithes of all that I possess." And the tax collector, standing afar off, would not so much as raise his eyes to heaven, but beat his breast, saying, "God, be merciful to me, a sinner!"

I tell you, this man went down to his house justified rather than the other; for everyone who exalts himself will be humbled, and he who humbles himself will be exalted.

Mt 7:3-5 And why do you look at the speck in your brother's eye, but do not consider the plank in your own eye? Or how can you say to your brother, "Let me remove the speck from your eye"; and look, a plank is in your own eye? Hypocrite! First remove the plank from your own eye, and then you will see clearly to remove the speck from your brother's eye.

Jn 7:24 Do not judge according to appearance, but judge with righteous judgment.

Ro 2:1-3 Therefore, you are inexcusable, O man, whoever you are who judge, for in whatever you judge another you condemn yourself; for you who judge practice the same things. But we know that the judgment of God is according to truth against those who practice such things. And do you think this, O man, you who judge those practicing such things, and doing the same, that you will escape the judgment of God?

Mt 7:1, 2 Judge not, that you be not judged. For with what judgment you judge, you will be judged; and with the measure you use, it will be measured back to you.

Ro 14:3 Let not him who eats despise him who does not eat, and let not him who does not eat judge him who eats; for God has received him.

Ro 14:13 Therefore let us not judge one another anymore, but rather resolve this, not to put a stumbling block or a cause to fall in our brother's way.

Tit 3:2a To speak evil of no one, to be peaceable, gentle, showing all humility to all men.

Persecution for Christ's Sake

There are many forms of religious persecution. When Christians stand up for the truth of God's Word in their communities, and with friends and relatives, persecution can range from rejection to isolation, even division and estranged relationships. However, Jesus talks about the kind of persecution that is promised to Christians who will stand for Him and will not deny Him.

In the western world we aren't as familiar with this type of persecution, but this certainly happens to our brothers and sisters in many countries of the world - Christians dying for their faith in Christ. It is important to stay close to the Lord and His Word, in meditation, for strengthening our spirits in order to be strong enough and humble enough to stand up for Jesus no matter what opposition comes against us, no matter the cost. Jesus was persecuted for speaking the truth and exposing the lies which both religion and the worldly people constantly affronted Him with.

* **2Tim 3:12** All who desire to live godly in Christ Jesus will suffer persecution.

* **Mt 5:10-12** Blessed are those who are persecuted for righteousness' sake, for theirs is the kingdom of heaven. Blessed are you, when men shall revile you, and persecute you, and shall say all manner of evil against you falsely, for my sake. Rejoice, and be exceeding glad: for great is your reward in heaven: for so persecuted they the prophets which were before you.

Mt 10:19, 20 But when they deliver you up, do not worry about how or what you should speak. For it will be given to you in that hour what you should speak; for it is not you who speak, but the Spirit of your Father who speaks in you.

Mt 10:22, 23a And you will be hated by all for My name's sake. But he who endures to the end will be saved. When they persecute you in this city, flee to another.

Mt 10:28 And do not fear those who kill the body but cannot kill the soul. But rather fear Him who is able to destroy both soul and body in hell.

Mt 24:8-10 All these are the beginning of sorrows. Then they will deliver you up to tribulation and kill you, and you will be

IX. RELIGIOSITY VS CHRISTIANITY

hated by all nations for My name's sake. And then many will be offended, will betray one another, and will hate one another.

Mk 13:11 But when they arrest you and deliver you up, do not worry beforehand, or premeditate what you will speak. But whatever is given you in that hour, speak that; for it is not you who speak, but the Holy Spirit.

Mk 15:10 For he knew that the chief priests had handed Him over because of envy.

Lk 6:22, 23 Blessed are you when men hate you, and when they exclude you, and revile you, and cast out your name as evil, for the Son of Man's sake. Rejoice in that day and leap for joy! For indeed your reward is great in heaven, for in like manner their fathers did to the prophets.

Mt 10:17, 18 But beware of men, for they will deliver you up to councils and scourge you in their synagogues; and you shall be brought before governors and kings for My sake, for a testimony against them and the Gentiles.

Jn 15:19, 20 If you were of the world, the world would love its own. Yet because you are not of the world, but I chose you out of the world, therefore the world hates you. Remember the word that I said to you, 'A servant is not greater than his master.' If they persecuted Me, they will also persecute you. If they have kept My word, they will keep yours also.

* **Jn 16:2** They will put you out of the synagogues; yes, the time is coming that whoever kills you will think that he offers God service.

Jn 16:33 These things I have spoken to you, that in Me you may have peace. In the world you will have tribulation; but be of good cheer, I have overcome the world.

* **Mt 5:44** But I say to you, love your enemies, bless those who curse you, do good to those who hate you, and pray for those who spitefully use you and persecute you.

Jn 17:14 I have given them Your word; and the world has hated them because they are not of the world, just as I am not of the world.

Acts 4:29 Now, Lord, look on their threats, and grant to Your servants that with all boldness they may speak Your word.

* **Phil 1:29** For to you it has been granted on behalf of Christ, not only to believe in Him, but also to suffer for His sake.

1Pt 3:14 But even if you should suffer for righteousness' sake, you are blessed. And do not be afraid of their threats, nor be troubled.

1Pt 4:16 Yet, if anyone suffers as a Christian, let him not be ashamed, but let him glorify God in this matter.

* **Rev 2:10** Do not fear any of those things which you are about to suffer. Indeed, the devil is about to throw some of you into prison, that you may be tested, and you will have tribulation ten days. Be faithful until death, and I will give you the crown of life.

* **Ro 8:31b** If God is for us, who can be against us?

* **Mt 10:23a** When they persecute you in this city, flee to another.

* **Lk 21:17-19** And you will be hated by all for My name's sake. But not a hair of your head shall be lost. By your patience possess your souls.

* **Jn 15:20** Remember the word that I said to you, 'A servant is not greater than his master.' If they persecuted Me, they will also persecute you. If they kept My word, they will keep yours also.

* **Acts 5:38b, 39** If this plan or this work is of men, it will come to nothing; but if it is of God, you cannot overthrow it—lest you even be found to fight against God.

X. WITNESSING OUR FAITH

Jesus said, *"Go into all the world and preach the gospel to every creature" (Mk 16:15-18)*. Our testimony is our greatest witness when telling others about our faith. Once we have been exposed to the light, to true love and truth, we feel compelled to talk about it! The Apostle Paul said, *"The love of God compels me" (2Cor 5:14-15)*. God's Spirit will show you those who are lost, and in your heart you will be drawn to bring them into God's Kingdom also. So witnessing is simply testifying of the great joy and the awesome change that has taken place in your heart. In any court of law, witnesses are some of the most powerful assets to any case, because they are a firsthand account. It is the same in God's Kingdom.

The Great Commission

The great commission that Jesus has left us is the privilege to share with others the good news that Christ has come to redeem mankind, meaning that anyone can live the full life of the kingdom now, through faith in Jesus. Plus, we get to be a light to the world and share His love and truth along with the joy, happiness and fulfilment that He brought into our hearts through our newborn nature. We get to share God's grace with everyone we meet, so they too can live as enlightened a life as we live. They too can enter and enjoy the kingdom of heaven now. Is there any greater calling in life? It is both the greatest opportunity and the greatest responsibility. Because if we don't, how else will they know?

The Bible says, *"Do not withhold good from those who deserve it when it's in your power to help them" (Pro 3:27)*. Every day God gives us opportunities to show kindness to people around us. Our choice is to be the light of the world or to be self-centered? Even a word of encouragement, a pat on the back, an errand done for them, any of those could mean a lot; it could mean God's love manifested.

We're all on a mission once we've come into God's kingdom. People say, "I work at a secular job." Actually, it's only secular if we don't bring God in it. But if we do, it becomes our mission. Since we are the light of the world, everyone we come in contact with is a 'divine appointment'.

Christian parents have one of the greatest missions ever given to man, because they're constantly imparting their values to their children. So, in many respects, we should all be in full-time ministry.

* **Mk 16:15-18** Go into all the world and preach the gospel to every creature. He who believes and is baptized will be saved; but he who does not believe will be condemned. And these signs will follow those who believe: In My name they will cast out demons; they will speak with new tongues; they will take up serpents; and if they drink anything deadly, it will by no means hurt them; they will lay hands on the sick, and they will recover.

* **Mt 28:19, 20** Go therefore and make disciples of all the nations, baptizing them in the name of the Father and of the Son and of the Holy Spirit, teaching them to observe all things that I have commanded you; and lo, I am with you always, even to the end of the age.

* **2Tim 2:2** And the things that you have heard from Me among many witnesses, commit these to faithful men who will be able to teach others also.

  Ro 10:14, 15 How then shall they call on Him in whom they have not believed? And how shall they believe in Him of whom they have not heard? And how shall they hear without a preacher? And how shall they preach unless they are sent? As it is written, 'How beautiful are the feet of those who preach the gospel of peace, who bring glad tidings of good things!'

* **Jn 15:8** By this My Father is glorified, that you bear much fruit; so you will be My disciples.

* **Eze 3:17-19** Son of man, I have made you a watchman for the house of Israel; therefore hear a word from My mouth, and give them warning from Me: When I say to the wicked, 'You shall surely die,' and you give him no warning, nor speak to warn the wicked from his wicked way, to save his life, that same wicked

man shall die in his iniquity; but his blood I will require at your hand. Yet, if you warn the wicked, and he does not turn from his wickedness, nor from his wicked way, he shall die in his iniquity; but you have delivered your soul.

* **Pr 11:30** The fruit of the righteous is a tree of life, and he who wins souls is wise.

* **Dan 12:3** Those who are wise shall shine like the brightness of the firmament, and those who turn many to righteousness like the stars forever and ever.

* **Mt 4:19** Then He said to them, "Follow Me, and I will make you fishers of men."

  Mk 16:20 And they went out and preached everywhere, the Lord working with them and confirming the word through the accompanying signs.

  Mk 8:35 For whoever desires to save his life will lose it, but whoever loses his life for My sake and the gospel's will save it.

* **Mt 9:37, 38** Then He said to His disciples, "The harvest truly is plentiful, but the laborers are few. Therefore pray the Lord of the harvest to send out laborers into His harvest."

  Lk 9:3-5 And He said to them, "Take nothing for the journey, neither staffs nor bag nor bread nor money; and do not have two tunics apiece. Whatever house you enter, stay there, and from there depart. And whoever will not receive you, when you go out of that city, shake off the very dust from your feet as a testimony against them."

  Lk 12:8, 9 Also I say to you, whoever confesses Me before men, him the Son of Man also will confess before the angels of God. But he who denies Me before men will be denied before the angels of God.

* **Jn 15:16** You did not choose Me, but I chose you and appointed you that you should go and bear fruit, and that your fruit should remain, that whatever you ask the Father in My name He may give you.

Jn 20:21 So Jesus said to them again, "Peace to you! As the Father has sent Me, I also send you."

* **Acts 5:42** Daily in the temple, and in every house, they did not cease teaching and preaching Jesus as the Christ.

* **2Tim 4:2a** Preach the word! Be ready in season and out of season.

Jn 21:16 He said to him again a second time, "Simon, son of Jonah, do you love Me?" He said to Him, "Yes, Lord; You know that I love You." He said to him, "Tend My sheep."

1Cor 3:6, 7 I planted, Apollos watered, but God gave the increase. So then neither he who plants is anything, nor he who waters, but God who gives the increase.

1Pt 5:2 Shepherd the flock of God which is among you, serving as overseers, not by compulsion but willingly, not for dishonest gain but eagerly.

* **1Cor 9:16** For if I preach the gospel, I have nothing to boast of, for necessity is laid upon me; yes, woe is me if I do not preach the gospel!

* **Lk 9:2** He sent them to preach the kingdom of God and to heal the sick.

* **Jn 6:27** Do not labor for the food which perishes, but for the food which endures to everlasting life, which the Son of Man will give you, because God the Father has set His seal on Him.

* **Mt 5:14, 15** You are the light of the world. A city that is set on a hill cannot be hidden. Nor do they light a lamp and put it under a basket, but on a lampstand, and it gives light to all who are in the house.

* **1Cor 2:4, 5** And my speech and my preaching were not with persuasive words of human wisdom, but in demonstration of the Spirit and of power, that your faith should not be in the wisdom of men but in the power of God.

X. WITNESSING OUR FAITH

* **1Pt 3:15b** Always be ready to give a defense to everyone who asks you a reason for the hope that is in you, with meekness and fear.

Unashamed Boldness and Conviction

This is one awesome gift that the Holy Spirit empowers us with: unashamed boldness. (See Acts 1:8). We have the conviction to speak out and to stand up for what we believe is right and true and loving, and that's why Christians must be bold in speaking out their faith unashamedly.

* **Acts 1:8** But you shall receive power when the Holy Spirit has come upon you; and you shall be witnesses to Me in Jerusalem, and in all Judea and Samaria, and to the end of the earth.

Mk 8:38 Whoever is ashamed of Me and My words in this adulterous and sinful generation, of him the Son of Man also will be ashamed when He comes in the glory of His Father with the holy angels.

Eph 6:19, 20 And for me, that utterance may be given to me, that I may open my mouth boldly to make known the mystery of the gospel, for which I am an ambassador in chains; that in it I may speak boldly, as I ought to speak.

Ps 119:46 I will speak of Your testimonies also before kings, and will not be ashamed.

Isa 40:9b Lift up your voice with strength, Lift it up, be not afraid; Say to the cities of Judah, "Behold your God!"

Isa 50:4a The Lord God has given Me the tongue of the learned, that I should know how to speak a word in season to him who is weary.

Jer 1:7 The Lord said to me, "Do not say, 'I am a youth,' for you shall go to all to whom I send you, and whatever I command you, you shall speak".

Mt 5:16 Let your light so shine before men, that they may see your good works and glorify your Father in heaven.

Lk 12:8 Also I say to you, whoever confesses Me before men, him the Son of Man also will confess before the angels of God.

* **Acts 4:13** Now when they saw the boldness of Peter and John, and perceived that they were uneducated and untrained men, they marveled and they realized that they had been with Jesus.

Acts 18:9b, 10 Do not be afraid, but speak, and do not keep silent; for I am with you, and no one will attack you to hurt you; for I have many people in this city.

Ro 1:16 For I am not ashamed of the gospel of Christ, for it is the power of God to salvation for everyone who believes

Tit 2:15 Speak these things, exhort, and rebuke with all authority. Let no one despise you.

Manifesting a True Christian Life

If you truly believe in something, it will show in the way you live and in your demeanor. Your belief becomes a conviction of the heart and you stand by it. So the life of a Christian is a manifestation, an example of faith lived out. It will show the world Who you're in love with! Most people will only believe the Bible if it's bound in shoe leather. In other words, they will only believe it if you live it, yourself. Once your heart has been filled with the love of God, you want to do unto others as has been done unto you. You want others to also partake of His loving kindness. It goes further than telling them about God's love. You can become the love of God expressed to them in many ways: helping, listening, understanding, forgiving, teaching, nurturing, and guiding, and the list goes on.

The Christian's Love for the World

Once you are born again, loving others is no longer a duty but a privilege. Once you realize how much you've been loved and how much love God has for every man and woman out there, it lights you up to witness His truth. It's His love that lights up our faith to share the good news. (See 2Cor 5:14a) You are your brother's keeper. Let's re-read the parable of the

X. WITNESSING OUR FAITH

good Samaritan. It applies to all of us. (See Lk 10: 25-37) The greatest form of love is our willingness to sacrifice our lives, which means putting others' needs before our own. Jesus said, *"Except the corn of wheat falls into the ground and dies, it abides alone, but if it dies it brings forth much fruit" (Jn 12:24)* and, *"Greater love has no man than this that he lay down his life for his friends" (Jn 15:13)*. We can measure love by our willingness to make sacrifices for others. And the greater the sacrifice, the deeper the love. Learning to win the spiritual warfare starts with daily choices like telling the truth, being unselfish, and being forgiving and loving. Jesus says, *"If any man will come after Me, let him deny himself and take up his cross" (Mt 16:24)*. We have to be willing to eliminate distractions, and not be entangled with the world. Paul said, *"No one engaged in warfare entangles himself with the affairs of this life, that he may please him who enlisted him as a soldier." (2Tim 2:4)*.

Lk 6:31-35 And just as you want men to do to you, you also do to them likewise. But if you love those who love you, what credit is that to you? For even sinners love those who love them. And if you do good to those who do good to you, what credit is that to you? For even sinners do the same. And if you lend to those from whom you hope to receive back, what credit is that to you? For even sinners lend to sinners to receive as much back. But love your enemies, do good, and lend, hoping for nothing in return; and your reward will be great, and you will be sons of the Most High. For He is kind to the unthankful and evil.

* **1Jn 3:16, 18** By this we know love, because He laid down His life for us. And we also ought to lay down our lives for the brethren. My little children, let us not love in word or in tongue, but in deed and in truth.

1Jn 4:20, 21 If someone says, 'I love God,' and hates his brother, he is a liar; for he who does not love his brother whom he has seen, how can he love God whom he has not seen? And this commandment we have from Him: that he who loves God must love his brother also.

Mt 5:43, 44, 46, 47 You have heard that it was said, 'You shall love your neighbor and hate your enemy.' But I say to you, love your enemies, bless those who curse you, do good to those who hate you, and pray for those who spitefully use you and persecute you. For if you love those who love you, what reward have you? Do not even the tax collectors do the same? And if you greet your brethren only, what do you do more than others? Do not even the tax collectors do so?

Mt 7:12 Therefore, whatever you want men to do to you, do also to them, for this is the law and the prophets.

* **Mt 22:37-40** You shall love the Lord your God with all your heart, with all your soul, and with all your mind. This is the first and great commandment. And the second is like it: You shall love your neighbor as yourself. On these two commandments hang all the law and the prophets.

Mt 25:35 For I was hungry and you gave Me food; I was thirsty and you gave Me drink; I was a stranger and you took Me in.

* **Jn 13:34, 35** A new commandment I give to you, that you love one another; as I have loved you, that you also love one another. By this all will know that you are My disciples, if you have love for one another.

* **Jn 15:13** Greater love has no one than this, than to lay down one's life for his friends.

Ro 12:10 Be kindly affectionate to one another with brotherly love, in honor giving preference to one another.

* **Ro 13:8** Owe no one anything except to love one another, for he who loves another has fulfilled the law.

Ro 13:10 Love does no harm to a neighbor; therefore love is the fulfillment of the law.

* **1Cor 13:4-8a** Love suffers long and is kind; love does not envy; love does not parade itself, is not puffed up; does not behave rudely, does not seek its own, is not provoked, thinks no evil; does not rejoice in iniquity, but rejoices in the truth; bears all

X. WITNESSING OUR FAITH

things, believes all things, hopes all things, endures all things. Love never fails.

* **1Cor 13:13** And now abide faith, hope, love, these three; but the greatest of these is love.
* **1Cor 16:14** Let all that you do be done with love.

  1Pt 1:22 Since you have purified your souls in obeying the truth through the Spirit in sincere love of the brethren, love one another fervently with a pure heart.

  Col 3:12-14 Therefore, as the elect of God, holy and beloved, put on tender mercies, kindness, humility, meekness, longsuffering; bearing with one another, and forgiving one another, if anyone has a complaint against another; even as Christ forgave you, so you also must do. But above all these things put on love, which is the bond of perfection.
* **Gal 5:14** For all the law is fulfilled in one word, even in this: You shall love your neighbor as yourself.
* **Gal 6:2** Bear one another's burdens, and so fulfill the law of Christ.
* **1Pt 4:8** Above all things have fervent love for one another, for love will cover a multitude of sins.

  1Jn 2:10 He who loves his brother abides in the light, and there is no cause for stumbling in him.
* **1Jn 4:7, 8** Beloved, let us love one another, for love is of God; and everyone who loves is born of God and knows God. He who does not love does not know God, for God is love.

  1Jn 4:11, 12 Beloved, if God so loved us, we also ought to love one another. No one has seen God at any time. If we love one another, God abides in us, and His love has been perfected in us.
* **Gal 5:13b** Through love serve one another..

  Eph 5:2a And walk in love, as Christ also has loved us and given Himself for us.

* **Mt 25:40b** Inasmuch as you did it to one of the least of these My brethren, you did it to Me.
* **Mt 7:12** Therefore, whatever you want men to do to you, do also to them, for this is the law and the prophets.

Let's keep Our Witness Simple

Paul the Apostle, who was one of the main teachers and preachers of the gospel, himself a former Pharisee and brilliant student of the old law, condemns any kind of intellectual deliberations that lead to confusion and arguments. To help avoid any arguments, it is important to share what God has given to you, from your heart. What you have lived in the Word, in the Spirit, is the most powerful aspect of passing on the simplicity of the gospel to someone else. In this way the scriptures come alive, because you are the proof!

Tit 3:9 But avoid foolish disputes, genealogies, contentions, and strivings about the law; for they are unprofitable and useless.

1Thes 2:4-6 But as we have been approved by God to be entrusted with the gospel, even so we speak, not as pleasing men, but God who tests our hearts. For neither at any time did we use flattering words, as you know, nor a cloak for covetousness—God is witness. Nor did we seek glory from men, either from you or from others, when we might have made demands as apostles of Christ.

2Cor 1:12 For our boasting is this: the testimony of our conscience that we conducted ourselves in the world in simplicity and godly sincerity, not with fleshly wisdom but by the grace of God, and more abundantly toward you.

Mt 5:16 Let your light so shine before men, that they may see your good works and glorify your Father in heaven.

1Cor 1:17 For Christ did not send me to baptize, but to preach the gospel, not with wisdom of words, lest the cross of Christ should be made of no effect.

X. WITNESSING OUR FAITH

1Cor 1:27-29 But God has chosen the foolish things of the world to put to shame the wise, and God has chosen the weak things of the world to put to shame the things which are mighty; and the base things of the world and the things which are despised God has chosen, and the things which are not, to bring to nothing the things that are, that no flesh should glory in His presence.

2Cor 3:12 Therefore, since we have such hope, we use great boldness of speech.

Unity amongst Believers

Jesus says that when two or three are gathered together in His name, He's there! There is so much power in unity and that is why the devil uses division to render ineffective the power that we could have as a united body of Christ. The entire body of Christian believers is the body of Christ. Denominations were never initiated by Jesus. We're supposed to all be one body. That is what is described in the Bible as the church. Not a building, not a denomination, but a body of believers. And Jesus insisted on our being united together as He is united with the Father. The Word says, *"When one member suffers, the whole body suffers" (1Cor 12:26)*.

We are told in Hebrews 10:25, *"Let us not forsake the assembling of ourselves together"*. There is great power in unity.

Meeting together for an hour or two for fellowship should be a genuine pleasure and relaxation! It should be a time to be renewed, re-inspired and fueled up for the work and strengthened for the battles in the days ahead!

For its first 200 years of existence, Christianity had no buildings, and Christians just met wherever they could. Jesus said, *"Wherever two or three are gathered together in My name, <u>there</u> am I in their midst!" (Mat 18:20)*. All throughout the New Testament times, the Church thrived and grew and got along fine without any church buildings or "houses of God"! The only meeting places that Christians had were their <u>homes</u>. Repeatedly the Apostle Paul refers to *"the church that is in your house"* (Rom 16:5; 1Corinthians 16:19; Colossians 4:15; Philemon 2).

Note that the house itself was not the Church, but the "church" met in their houses!

The word "church" as translated from Ekklesia in Greek, literally means "the called out or chosen ones" or "the body of believers"! God's true and living Church are the genuine Christian believers in God who follow Jesus, the born-again, saved body of Christ. Not a building or any particular denomination!

Jn 17:21 That they all may be one, as You, Father, are in Me, and I in You; that they also may be one in Us, that the world may believe that You sent Me.

1Cor 12:14-18 For in fact the body is not one member but many. If the foot should say, "Because I am not a hand, I am not of the body," is it therefore not of the body? And if the ear should say, "Because I am not an eye, I am not of the body," is it therefore not of the body? If the whole body were an eye, where would be the hearing? If the whole were hearing, where would be the smelling? But now God has set the members, each one of them, in the body just as He pleased.

* **Ro 12:5** We, being many, are one body in Christ, and individually members of one another.

* **1Cor 1:10** Now I plead with you, brethren, by the name of our Lord Jesus Christ, that you all speak the same thing, and that there be no divisions among you, but that you be perfectly joined together in the same mind and in the same judgment.

* **Ecc 4:9, 10, 12** Two are better than one, because they have a good reward for their labor. For if they fall, one will lift up his companion. But woe to him who is alone when he falls, for he has no one to help him up. Though one may be overpowered by another, two can withstand him. And a threefold cord is not quickly broken.

* **Mt 18:19, 20** If two of you agree on earth concerning anything that they ask, it will be done for them by My Father in heaven.

X. WITNESSING OUR FAITH

For where two or three are gathered together in My name, I am there in the midst of them.

* **Acts 2:44, 45** Now all who believed were together, and had all things in common, and sold their possessions and goods, and divided them among all, as anyone had need.

  Acts 4:32a Now the multitude of those who believed were of one heart and one soul.

* **Ro 14:19** Therefore let us pursue the things which make for peace and the things by which one may edify another.

  1Cor 14:26 How is it then, brethren? Whenever you come together, each of you has a psalm, has a teaching, has a tongue, has a revelation, has an interpretation. Let all things be done for edification.

  Eph 4:3 Endeavoring to keep the unity of the Spirit in the bond of peace.

  Phil 1:27b Stand fast in one spirit, with one mind striving together for the faith of the gospel.

  Phil 2:2 Fulfill my joy by being like-minded, having the same love, being of one accord, of one mind.

* **1Jn 1:7a** If we walk in the light as He is in the light, we have fellowship with one another.

* **Ps 133:1** Behold, how good and how pleasant it is for brethren to dwell together in unity!

Walking in Humility

Humility is the quality of putting the needs of another person before your own, and thinking of others first. Also, it means not drawing attention to yourself and it can mean acknowledging that you are not always right. Humility doesn't mean we think less of ourselves, rather, we think of ourselves less. So, 'walking in humility' would be making an effort to live by the Godly principles of putting other peoples' needs, ideas and opinions before our own.

The Word says that God resists the proud, but gives grace to the humble. The goal is for us to walk in humility. Humility is being "other people centered", which is to fulfill the law of love. The humble receives grace. We are supposed to submit ourselves to God, humble ourselves before God, resist pride, not to lean to our own understanding. That's the path of humility.

Any and all sins have their root in pride. Satan fell because of pride. (See Is 14:12-16) The proud puts himself first. Therefore, he is selfish, stubborn, will not forgive, but will keep a grudge, which makes him judgmental. He will easily gossip and slander to boost his ego. He is his own legend. He values his own opinion more than others' and therefore manipulates and even intimidates others.

The proud are easily angry. There are so many pitfalls to pride. The proud is the most insecure of all people. We think that pride makes us bigger, but in actual fact it diminishes us. It diminishes our capacity to give and to receive. The Bible says that "pride comes before a fall". (See Pr 16:18) It is often sneaky because it hides in false humility. He is proud to be humble; holy humble, and proud of it. And because he depends on his own strength, he cannot cast his burdens on the Lord and depend utterly on Him. Pride is very dangerous in the Lord's kingdom.

Lk 14:10 But when you are invited, go and sit down in the lowest place, so that when he who invited you comes he may say to you, 'Friend, go up higher.'

Lk 16:15 And He said to them, "You are those who justify yourselves before men, but God knows your hearts. For what is highly esteemed among men is an abomination in the sight of God.

Col 3:12 Therefore, as the elect of God, holy and beloved, put on tender mercies, kindness, humility, meekness, longsuffering.

Jam 4:6 But He gives more grace. Therefore He says: "God resists the proud, but gives grace to the humble."

* **Mt 23:12b** He who humbles himself will be exalted.

X. WITNESSING OUR FAITH

Ps 25:9 The humble He guides in justice, and the humble He teaches His way.

Ps 37:11 But the meek shall inherit the earth, and shall delight themselves in the abundance of peace.

Pr 15:33 The fear of the Lord is the instruction of wisdom, and before honor is humility.

Pr 22:4 By humility and the fear of the Lord are riches and honor and life.

Mt 5:5 Blessed are the meek, for they shall inherit the earth.

Mt 18:4 Therefore whoever humbles himself as this little child is the greatest in the kingdom of heaven.

Lk 1:52 He has put down the mighty from their thrones, and exalted the lowly.

* **2Cor 10:17** But he who glories, let him glory in the Lord.

Phil 2:5-8 Let this mind be in you which was also in Christ Jesus, who, being in the form of God, did not consider it robbery to be equal with God, but made Himself of no reputation, taking the form of a bondservant, and coming in the likeness of men. And being found in appearance as a man, He humbled Himself and became obedient to the point of death, even the death of the cross.

Jam 4:10 Humble yourselves in the sight of the Lord, and He will lift you up.

Ps 138:6 Though the Lord is on high, yet He regards the lowly; but the proud He knows from afar.

Mic 6:8 He has shown you, O man, what is good; and what does the Lord require of you but to do justly, to love mercy, and to walk humbly with your God?

1Sam 2:3 Talk no more so very proudly; let no arrogance come from your mouth, for the Lord is the God of knowledge; and by Him actions are weighed.

* **Dan 4:37b** Those who walk in pride He is able to put down.

Ps 51:17 The sacrifices of God are a broken spirit, a broken and a contrite heart— These, O God, You will not despise.

Ps 10:4 The wicked in his proud countenance does not seek God; God is in none of his thoughts.

Pr 3:7 Do not be wise in your own eyes; fear the Lord and depart from evil.

Pr 8:13 The fear of the Lord is to hate evil; pride and arrogance and the evil way and the perverse mouth I hate.

* **Pr 11:2** When pride comes, then comes shame; but with the humble is wisdom.

* **Pr 16:18** Pride goes before destruction, and a haughty spirit before a fall.

Pr 26:12 Do you see a man wise in his own eyes? There is more hope for a fool than for him.

Pr 27:2 Let another man praise you, and not your own mouth; a stranger, and not your own lips.

Pr 29:23 A man's pride will bring him low, but the humble in spirit will retain honor.

* **Mt 23:12a** Whoever exalts himself will be humbled.

Jn 12:43 For they loved the praise of men more than the praise of God.

Ro 12:3a To everyone who is among you, not to think of himself more highly than he ought to think.

1Cor 10:12 Therefore let him who thinks he stands take heed lest he fall.

* **1Pt 5:5-7** Likewise you younger people, submit yourselves to your elders. Yes, all of you be submissive to one another, and be clothed with humility, for God resists the proud, But gives grace to the humble. Therefore humble yourselves under the mighty hand of God, that He may exalt you in due time.

1Jn 2:16 For all that is in the world—the lust of the flesh, the lust of the eyes, and the pride of life—is not of the Father but is of the world.

* **Phil 2:3** Let nothing be done through selfish ambition or conceit, but in lowliness of mind let each esteem others better than himself.
* **Eph 6:6** Not with eye service, as men-pleasers, but as bondservants of Christ, doing the will of God from the heart.

XI. FINANCES OF THE KINGDOM

Many of the parables that Jesus taught had to do with finances. He is well aware of our need for money, enough to teach us how to handle finances. But He also knows that finances can become a god (Mammon) and therefore warns us not to focus on money nor to worry about money, but rather to seek first the Kingdom of God. He wants us to put Him first, and that includes tithing and giving.

There are five main principles to handling finances in God's kingdom that will insure our well-being and even our prosperity. But they require discipline. They are:
1) Live on a budget; live within your means (Lk 14:28).
2) Avoid debts; don't spend impulsively (Pro 22:7).
3) Mind your company of friends; you become like those you frequent (1 Cor 15:33).
4) Plan and save; accumulation is created by savings. (Pro 21:20).
5) Be cheerfully generous (2 Cor 9:7).

Lk 14:28. For which of you, intending to build a tower, does not sit down first, and counts the cost, whether he has sufficient to finish it?

Pr 22:7 The rich rules over the poor, and the borrower is servant to the lender.

1Cor 15:33 Do not be deceived: Evil company corrupts good habits.

Pr 21:20 There is desirable treasure, and oil in the dwelling of the wise, but a foolish man squanders it.

2Cor 9:7b For God loves a cheerful giver.

Mt 6:31-33 Therefore do not worry, saying, "What shall we eat?" or "What shall we drink?" or "What shall we wear?" For after all these things the Gentiles seek. For your heavenly Father knows that you need all these things. But seek first the kingdom

XI. FINANCES OF THE KINGDOM

of God and His righteousness, and all these things shall be added to you.

Pr 3:9, 10 Honor the Lord with your possessions, and with the first fruits of all your increase; so your barns will be filled with plenty, and your vats will overflow with new wine.

Jam 1:17 Every good gift and every perfect gift is from above, and comes down from the Father of lights, with whom there is no variation or shadow of turning.

Lk 12:23-34 Life is more than food, and the body is more than clothing. Consider the ravens, for they neither sow nor reap, which have neither storehouse nor barn; and God feeds them. Of how much more value are you than the birds? And which of you by worrying can add one cubit to his stature? If you then are not able to do the least, why are you anxious for the rest? Consider the lilies, how they grow: they neither toil nor spin; and yet I say to you, even Solomon in all his glory was not arrayed like one of these. If then God so clothes the grass, which today is in the field and tomorrow is thrown into the oven, how much more will He clothe you, O you of little faith? And do not seek what you should eat or what you should drink, nor have an anxious mind. For all these things the nations of the world seek after, and your Father knows that you need these things. But seek the kingdom of God, and all these things shall be added to you. Do not fear, little flock, for it is your Father's good pleasure to give you the kingdom. Sell what you have and give alms; provide yourselves money bags which do not grow old, a treasure in the heavens that does not fail, where no thief approaches nor moth destroys. For where your treasure is, there your heart will be also.

Lk 14:28 For which of you, intending to build a tower, does not sit down first and count the cost, whether he has enough to finish it.

Promises of Blessings

God's blessings are bestowed upon His sons and daughters in many ways. Just think of any area of your life where you would need to feel His Fatherly hand extending a blessing, that is in every area of our lives! Through His Word He teaches us how to secure those blessings for the material, physical, financial, emotional and social needs that we have in our daily lives. But God expects our love and devotion before He bestows blessings upon us. Obedience proceeds blessings. And our faith in receiving is activated through reading and obeying the Word, then we can expect and claim those blessings, which He so abundantly promised.

Once we fully comprehend who we are as sons and daughters of God, and truly believe in His unending love for us, we can claim blessings all through life. He has <u>not</u> promised us wealth, but rather the power to <u>create</u> wealth if we look to Him and depend on Him (Deut 8:18).

Deut 28:2-6, 8, 11, 12 And all these blessings shall come upon you and overtake you, because you obey the voice of the Lord your God: Blessed shall you be in the city, and blessed shall you be in the country. Blessed shall be the fruit of your body, the produce of your ground and the increase of your herds, the increase of your cattle and the offspring of your flocks. Blessed shall be your basket and your kneading bowl. Blessed shall you be when you come in, and blessed shall you be when you go out. The Lord will command the blessing on you in your storehouses and in all to which you set your hand, and He will bless you in the land which the Lord your God is giving you. And the Lord will grant you plenty of goods, in the fruit of your body, in the increase of your livestock, and in the produce of your ground, in the land of which the Lord swore to your fathers to give you. The Lord will open to you His good treasure, the heavens, to give the rain to your land in its season, and to bless all the work of your hand. You shall lend to many nations, but you shall not borrow.

XI. FINANCES OF THE KINGDOM

Deut 8:18 And you shall remember the Lord your God, for it is He who gives you power to get wealth, that He may establish His covenant which He swore to your fathers, as it is this day.

* **Josh 1:8** This book of the law shall not depart from your mouth, but you shall meditate in it day and night, that you may observe to do according to all that is written in it. For then you will make your way prosperous, and then you will have good success.

Gen 9:3 Every moving thing that lives shall be food for you. I have given you all things, even as the green herbs.

2Chr 26:5b And as long as he sought the Lord, God made him prosper.

* **Ps 23:1** The Lord is my shepherd; I shall not want.

Ps 34:10 The young lions lack and suffer hunger; but those who seek the Lord shall not lack any good thing.

* **Ps 84:11b** The Lord will give grace and glory; no good thing will He withhold from those who walk uprightly.

Ps 128:1, 2 Blessed is every one who fears the Lord, who walks in His ways. When you eat the labor of your hands, you shall be happy, and it shall be well with you.

Pr 10:3a The Lord will not allow the righteous soul to famish.

Pr 10:22 The blessing of the Lord makes one rich, and He adds no sorrow with it.

Pr 13:22 A good man leaves an inheritance to his children's children, but the wealth of the sinner is stored up for the righteous.

Lk 12:24 Consider the ravens, for they neither sow nor reap, which have neither storehouse nor barn, and God feeds them.

Ps 37:3 Trust in the Lord, and do good; dwell in the land, and feed on His faithfulness.

Ps 68:19a Blessed be the Lord, Who daily loads us with benefits.

Lk 22:35 And He said to them, "When I sent you without a money bag, knapsack, and sandals, did you lack anything?" They said, "Nothing."

Ro 8:32 He who did not spare His own Son, but delivered Him up for us all, how shall He not with Him also freely give us all things?

1Cor 9:11 If we have sown spiritual things for you, is it a great thing if we reap your material things?

* **1Cor 10:10** Nor complain, as some of them also complained, and were destroyed by the destroyer.

* **Phil 2:14** Do all things without complaining and disputing.

* **Phil 4:11b** I have learned in whatever state I am, to be content.

* **Ro 9:20** Who are you to reply against God? Will the thing formed say to him who formed it, "Why have you made me like this"?

* **Mt 6:33** But seek first the kingdom of God and His righteousness, and all these things shall be added to you.

* **Jam 4:2b, 3** Yet you do not have because you do not ask. You ask and do not receive, because you ask amiss, that you may spend it on your pleasures.

* **1Cor 9:14** Even so the Lord has commanded that those who preach the gospel should live from the gospel.

* **Mt 6:25, 26** Therefore I say to you, do not worry about your life, what you will eat or what you will drink; nor about your body, what you will put on. Is not life more than food and the body more than clothing? Look at the birds of the air, for they neither sow nor reap nor gather into barns; yet your heavenly Father feeds them. Are you not of more value than they?

* **Mal 3:10** "Bring all the tithes into the storehouse, that there may be food in My house, and try Me now in this," says the Lord of hosts, "if I will not open for you the windows of heaven and pour out for you such blessing that there will not be room enough to receive it."

***Phil 4:19** My God shall supply all your need according to His riches in glory by Christ Jesus.

XI. FINANCES OF THE KINGDOM

Stewardship and Integrity

God can lavish upon us so many blessings, but he is not wasteful. Remember after the miracles of the loaves and fishes, they gathered all of the leftovers. That's called stewardship and caring about the blessings that God gives us.

He also expects us to walk in integrity. The Bible refers to integrity as "the pure in heart" or "blameless". It doesn't mean sinless or perfect. God is more interested in the direction of our hearts, in our motives more than in what we do. He wants us to be true through and through. He's interested in building our character. Our lives should not be departmentalized whereby we are one person in career, a different person in family, yet a different person with friends, and again different in business. Integrity means you are who you are before whoever. You wear no mask.

Your reputation before man is the same as it is before God. *"He who walks with integrity walks securely, but he who perverts his ways will become known" (Pro 10:9)*. The person who walks in integrity speaks truth from his heart, he refuses to slander others, will not listen to gossip, will not cast slur on his fellow man, will honor those who fear the Lord and will keep his promise even if it hurts him. He will also lend money freely without interest. (See Ex 22:25) and will not be bribed by money, compliments or favors. (See Pro 6:25) God expects every area of our life to be treated with the same excellence of character. It is an excellent spirit that gets promotion. (See Luke 16:11)

Joseph was excellent even in the worst of situations. He was serving God not Potiphar; he had an excellent spirit in jail which led him to be in charge of the jail. He had an excellent spirit when he was second in command of the mightiest nation on earth. God is looking for the right attitude to promote. He will use anyone with the right attitude. (See Ps 75:6, 7). It is God who promotes. And He gives it to the humble and to the faithful. God is no respecter of persons.

Daniel also was faithful to God from his youth and consequently God gave him favor and wisdom above all sages.

So it doesn't all have to do with how smart we are, or how educated we are, but with our excellence of spirit. (See 1 Cor 1:26)

Col 3:23 And whatever you do, do it heartily, as to the Lord and not to men.

Eph 6:6 Not with eye service, as men-pleasers, but as bondservants of Christ, doing the will of God from the heart.

Pr 18:9 He who is slothful in his work is a brother to him who is a great destroyer.

Mal 3:8-10 Will a man rob God? Yet you have robbed Me! But you say, 'In what way have we robbed You?' In tithes and offerings. You are cursed with a curse for you have robbed Me even this whole nation. Bring all the tithes into the storehouse, that there may be food in My house, and try Me now in this, says the Lord of hosts, if I will not open for you the windows of heaven and pour out for you such blessing that there will not be room enough to receive it.

Pr 10:8 The wise in heart will receive commands, but a prating fool will fall.

Pr 11:13 A talebearer reveals secrets, but he who is of a faithful spirit conceals a matter.

Ps 37:21 The wicked borrows and does not repay, but the righteous shows mercy and gives.

Ro 13:7 Render therefore to all their due: taxes to whom taxes are due, customs to whom customs, fear to whom fear, honor to whom honor.

Ps 15:4b He who swears to his own hurt and does not change.

Pr 2:7 He stores up sound wisdom for the upright; He is a shield to those who walk uprightly.

Pr 11:3 The integrity of the upright will guide them, but the perversity of the unfaithful will destroy them.

Pr 10:9 He who walks with integrity walks securely, but he who perverts his ways will become known.

XI. FINANCES OF THE KINGDOM

Pr 20:7 The righteous man walks in his integrity; his children are blessed after him.

* **Mt 25:23** Well done, good and faithful servant; you have been faithful over a few things, I will make you ruler over many things. Enter into the joy of your lord.

* **Lk 16:10** He who is faithful in what is least is faithful also in much; and he who is unjust in what is least is unjust also in much.

* **Ro 12:11** Not lagging in diligence, fervent in spirit, serving the Lord.

* **1Cor 4:2** It is required in stewards that one be found faithful.

2Chr 31:21 And in every work that he began in the service of the house of God, in the law and in the commandment, to seek his God, he did it with all his heart. So he prospered.

Pr 10:4 He who has a slack hand becomes poor, but the hand of the diligent makes rich.

Pr 10:5 He who gathers in summer is a wise son; he who sleeps in harvest is a son who causes shame.

Pr 13:4 The soul of a lazy man desires, and has nothing; but the soul of the diligent shall be made rich.

Pr 22:29 Do you see a man who excels in his work? He will stand before kings; he will not stand before unknown men.

* **Pr 28:20a** A faithful man will abound with blessings.

Pr 31:27 She watches over the ways of her household, and does not eat the bread of idleness.

Pr 13:4 The soul of a lazy man desires, and has nothing; But the soul of the diligent shall be made rich.

Ecc 10:18 Because of laziness the building decays, and through idleness of hands the house leaks.

2Thes 3:10b We commanded you this: if anyone will not work, neither shall he eat.

Mt 25:29 For to everyone who has, more will be given, and he will have abundance; but from him who does not have, even what he has will be taken away.

* **Rev 2:10** Do not fear any of those things which you are about to suffer. Indeed, the devil is about to throw some of you into prison, that you may be tested, and you will have tribulation ten days. Be faithful until death, and I will give you the crown of life.

* **Rev 3:11b** Hold fast what you have, that no one may take your crown.

* **Gal 6:9** And let us not grow weary while doing good, for in due season we shall reap if we do not lose heart.

* **Eph 5:16** Redeeming the time, because the days are evil.

Giving

The more we realize that <u>all</u> that we have received came from a loving heavenly Father, the easier it becomes to give; then tithing becomes a gesture of appreciation, and giving to others an extension of His love. We don't give out of our wallet, but out of His.

God is a giver and wants to bless people. So the more we give to others, the more He gives to us so that His love continues flowing through us. He does want to bless us financially, but He wants us to share the blessings that He gives us. He wants to prosper us so that we can give more.

There's a danger to prosperity. It can easily lead to complacency and lack of dependence on God. God is a giver and He wants us to be givers too. Jesus said, *"He who has two tunics, let him give to him who has none; and he who has food, let him do likewise,"* and *"go sell what you have and give to the poor, and you will have treasure in heaven"*. *"Do not seek what you are to eat or drink." "Seek not for yourself treasures on earth." (Lk 3:11; Mt 19:21; Lk 12:29; Mt 6:19, 20)* Also, when you give to the poor, it is like lending to the <u>Lord</u>, and the Lord will pay you back. (See Pro 19:17)

XI. FINANCES OF THE KINGDOM

There is another aspect to giving that needs to be highlighted. Paul talks a lot about his financial partners as his team. There is a "good reward" for those who partner with those who are on the frontlines. Jesus said, *"Where your treasure is there your heart will also be."* That means that we can move our heart's treasure by simply investing where it's most important and fruitful, in the actual preaching of the gospel and the making of disciples. When we support the works of God, He blesses us and the works of our hands. The law of generosity is you always reap more than you sow. We must plant by faith not by feelings.

* **Lk 6:38** Give, and it will be given to you: good measure, pressed down, shaken together, and running over will be put into your bosom. For with the same measure that you use, it will be measured back to you.

  Lk 3:11 He answered and said to them, "He who has two tunics, let him give to him who has none; and he who has food, let him do likewise."

  Mt 19:21 Jesus said to him, "If you want to be perfect, go, sell what you have and give to the poor, and you will have treasure in heaven; and come, follow Me".

* **Acts 20:35b** It is more blessed to give than to receive.

* **2Cor 9:6, 7** He who sows sparingly will also reap sparingly, and he who sows bountifully will also reap bountifully. So let each one give as he purposes in his heart, not grudgingly or of necessity; for God loves a cheerful giver.

  Deut 15:7, 8a, 10 If there is among you a poor man of your brethren, within any of the gates in your land which the Lord your God is giving you, you shall not harden your heart nor shut your hand from your poor brother. But you shall open your hand wide to him. You shall surely give to him, and your heart should not be grieved when you give to him, because for this thing the Lord your God will bless you in all your works and in all to which you put your hand.

* **Ps 41:1** Blessed is he who considers the poor; the Lord will deliver him in time of trouble.
* **Pr 3:27** Do not withhold good from those to whom it is due, when it is in the power of your hand to do so.

  Pr 11:24, 25 There is one who scatters, yet increases more; and there is one who withholds more than is right, but it leads to poverty. The generous soul will be made rich, and he who waters will also be watered himself.
* **Pr 19:17** He who has pity on the poor lends to the Lord, and He will pay back what he has given.

  Pr 28:16b He who hates covetousness will prolong his days.
* **Mt 5:42** Give to him who asks you, and from him who wants to borrow from you do not turn away.
* **Mt 10:8b** Freely you have received, freely give.
* **Mt 25:40b** Inasmuch as you did it to one of the least of these My brethren, you did it to Me.

  Phil 2:4 Let each of you look out not only for his own interests, but also for the interests of others.
* **1Jn 3:17, 18** Whoever has this world's goods, and sees his brother in need, and shuts up his heart from him, how does the love of God abide in him? My little children, let us not love in word or in tongue, but in deed and in truth.

XII. THE POWER OF OUR WORDS

It is through the spoken Word of God that God created the world. It is also through our speaking that we create our own world. Out of our mouth proceed blessings or curses. They give life or they take away life. When Adam ate of the tree of knowledge of good and evil, he empowered evil in his life and in his mouth. By losing his connection with the creator of life, he made connection with death.

However, even though born again, our tongue is not yet tamed into the new creature, the same as our mind. James says, *"It is an unruly member" (Jam 3:8)*. People who constantly curse their situation and circumstances and people around them end up living a cursed life. James says that our words are the actual <u>rudder</u> of our destiny. So there is a lot of power in our words, the power of life or death.

Authority Through Spoken Words

There are only a few times in the Bible where Jesus actually "marveled". One of these times is when a centurion who felt unworthy for Jesus to come into his house and heal his servant, said, *"Just speak the Word only" (Mt 8:8-13.)* Jesus was so amazed that even a man of the world had understood the concept of authority through the spoken Word.

It is our word spoken to different situations that actually has the authority to change things. That's also how you empower your negative thoughts, by <u>saying</u> your unbelief. Jesus said, *"Take no thought 'saying'" (Mat 6:25)*. You actually empower what you say. Your mouth spits out seeds of life or of death. And your mind becomes the ground for seeds. It goes with everything you take in; TV, news, conversations, books, etc. Read the Word of God whose seed is powerful and incorruptible.

Jam 3:5, 6, 8 Even so the tongue is a little member and boasts great things. See how great a forest a little fire kindles! And the tongue is a fire, a world of iniquity. The tongue is so set among our members that it defiles the whole body, and sets on fire the course of nature; and it is set on fire by hell. But no man can tame the tongue. It is an unruly evil, full of deadly poison.

Pr 18:21 Death and life are in the power of the tongue, and those who love it will eat its fruit.

Jam 3:11, 12 Does a spring send forth fresh water and bitter from the same opening? Can a fig tree, my brethren, bear olives, or a grapevine bear figs? Thus no spring yields both salt water and fresh.

Mt 15:16-20 So Jesus said, "Are you also still without understanding? Do you not yet understand that whatever enters the mouth goes into the stomach and is eliminated? But those things which proceed out of the mouth come from the heart, and they defile a man. For out of the heart proceed evil thoughts, murders, adulteries, fornications, thefts, false witness, and blasphemies. These are the things which defile a man, but to eat with unwashed hands does not defile a man."

* **Eph 4:29** Let no corrupt word proceed out of your mouth, but what is good for necessary edification, that it may impart grace to the hearers.

   1Cor 15:33 Do not be deceived. Evil company corrupts good habits.

   Pr 23:7a For as he thinks in his heart, so is he.

* **Mt 12:34b** Out of the abundance of the heart the mouth speaks.

   Ps 39:1a I said, "I will guard my ways, lest I sin with my tongue; I will restrain my mouth with a muzzle.

   Pr 13:3 He who guards his mouth preserves his life, but he who opens wide his lips shall have destruction.

   Mk 11:23 For assuredly, I say to you, whoever says to this mountain, be removed and be cast into the sea, and does not doubt in his heart, but believes that those things he says will be done, he will have whatever he says.

* **Mt 12:36, 37** But I say to you that for every idle word men may speak, they will give account of it in the day of judgment. For

by your words you will be justified, and by your words you will be condemned.

* **2Tim 2:16** Shun profane and idle babblings, for they will increase to more ungodliness.

The Uncontrolled Mouth

Learning to control our tongue (words) is as important as renewing our mind and keeping our thoughts into captivity to the obedience of God's Word. The Bible says that an uncontrolled tongue (speech) is as a city broken down and without walls. (See Pr 25:28) As our minds are renewed, our tongue will speak more out of the "abundance of our heart".

Below are more scriptures regarding anger and strife, gossiping and lying, judging and criticizing, bitterness vs forgiveness, as well as the power of kind words and encouragement, which are important to know as they outline principles and laws of God to abide by.

Power of the Spoken Word

We must verbally stand against our fears, lies, death, and worry spoken against you. We are affected by the words we hear. We are also affected by words spoken about ourselves.

Quantum physics has proven that words have the power to make you sick or healthy. Your words have creative power. You have the power to speak things into existence. No word from God is without fulfillment. With God all things are possible.

Anger and Strife

Anger is a sin when it is directed at people. Paul says that *"we should not let the sun go down on our anger" (Eph 4:26),* but it doesn't mean you can be angry and mean all day, for as long as you repent before you go to bed. Rather it refers to our anger against the devil and the works of the devil. We should not let the sun go down on our wrath against the enemy. We should stay stirred up against the works of the devil as Jesus did. But being angry against people is a sign of self-righteousness and pride, and therefore not of the Lord. There's a big cost to anger. When you let anger take control, you're going to cause irreparable damage. When you lose your temper, you always lose. You may lose someone's respect, the love of your family, your health, or even your job.

We think we get the short-term payoff, but in the long run, anger always produces more anger, more apathy, and more alienation. How many kids have become alienated from a parent because of out-of-control anger? Anger destroys relationships faster than anything else. How many folks have been torn apart from a boyfriend, a girlfriend, a husband, a wife, or a friend because somebody lost their cool? Anger against people is never the right kind of anger.

Hurt people hurt people. You can't think that if you pour out your anger on people, it'll be done and over with. No, you're only rehearsing for the next time. It is rooted deep in pride, the same as bitterness and has to be uprooted.

Jam 3:16 For where envy and self-seeking exist, confusion and every evil thing are there.

* **Phil 2:3** Let nothing be done through selfish ambition or conceit, but in lowliness of mind let each esteem others better than himself.

Jam 1:26 If anyone among you thinks he is religious, and does not bridle his tongue but deceives his own heart, this one's religion is useless.

Pr 14:29 He who is slow to wrath has great understanding. But he who is impulsive exalts folly.

Pr 16:32 He who is slow to anger is better than the mighty, and he who rules his spirit than he who takes a city.

Pr 26:21 As charcoal is to burning coals, and wood to fire, so is a contentious man to kindle strife.

Pr 28:25a He who is of a proud heart stirs up strife.

XII. THE POWER OF OUR WORDS

Pr 29:20 Do you see a man hasty in his words? There is more hope for a fool than for him.

Pr 29:22 An angry man stirs up strife, and a furious man abounds in transgression.

Ecc 4:6 Better a handful with quietness than both hands full, together with toil and grasping for the wind.

Ecc 7:8, 9 The end of a thing is better than its beginning; The patient in spirit is better than the proud in spirit. Do not hasten in your spirit to be angry, for anger rests in the bosom of fools.

Pr 17:14 The beginning of strife is like releasing water; therefore stop contention before a quarrel starts.

Pr 18:13 He who answers a matter before he hears it, it is folly and shame to him.

Pr 20:3 It is honorable for a man to stop striving, since any fool can start a quarrel.

Pr 25:8 Do not go hastily to court; for what will you do in the end when your neighbor has put you to shame?

Pr 15:18 A wrathful man stirs up strife, but he who is slow to anger allays contention.

Pr 15:1b Harsh word stirs up anger.

Pr 10:19b He who restrains his lips is wise.

Pr 11:12b A man of understanding holds his peace.

1Pt 3:9a Not returning evil for evil or reviling for reviling, but on the contrary, blessing.

Pr 17:27, 28 He who has knowledge spares his words, and a man of understanding is of a calm spirit. Even a fool is counted wise when he holds his peace; when he shuts his lips, he is considered perceptive.

Pr 21:23 Whoever guards his mouth and tongue keeps his soul from troubles.

* **Jam 1:19** So then, my beloved brethren, let every man be swift to hear, slow to speak, slow to wrath.

Gossiping and Lying

Pr 24:28 Do not be a witness against your neighbor without cause, for would you deceive with your lips?

Pr 10:18 Whoever hides hatred has lying lips, and whoever spreads slander is a fool.

Pr 25:9 Debate your case with your neighbor, and do not disclose the secret to another;

Pr 26:20 Where there is no wood, the fire goes out; and where there is no talebearer, strife ceases.

*Pr 29:11 A fool vents all his feelings, but a wise man holds them back.

Pr 30:32 If you have been foolish in exalting yourself, or if you have devised evil, put your hand on your mouth.

Pr 12:22 Lying lips are an abomination to the Lord.

Pr 16:28b A whisperer separates the best of friends.

Pr 25:18 A man who bears false witness against his neighbor is like a club, a sword, and a sharp arrow.

Ecc 10:20 Do not curse the king, even in your thought; Do not curse the rich, even in your bedroom; For a bird of the air may carry your voice, and a bird in flight may tell the matter.

Judging and Criticizing

Mt 7:1, 2 Judge not, that you be not judged. For with what judgment you judge, you will be judged; and with the measure you use, it will be measured back to you.

Mt 7:3-5 And why do you look at the speck in your brother's eye, but do not consider the plank in your own eye? Or how can you say to your brother, 'Let me remove the speck from your eye'; and look, a plank is in your own eye? Hypocrite! First remove the plank from your own eye, and then you will see clearly to remove the speck from your brother's eye.

Jn 7:24 Do not judge according to appearance, but judge with righteous judgment.

Ro 2:1-3 Therefore you are inexcusable, O man, whoever you are who judge, for in whatever you judge another you condemn yourself; for you who judge practice the same things. But we know that the judgment of God is according to truth against those who practice such things. And do you think this, O man, you who judge those practicing such things, and doing the same, that you will escape the judgment of God?

Ro 14:3 Let not him who eats despise him who does not eat, and let not him who does not eat judge him who eats; for God has received him.

Ro 14:13 Let us not judge one another anymore, but rather resolve this, not to put a stumbling block or a cause to fall in our brother's way.

Bitterness vs Forgiveness

When you are hurt, you operate in feelings. Bitterness blames. Unfortunately, psychology will only help you find who to blame, but God will teach you how to heal. Bitterness oftentimes distorts the truth in order to justify its hurt. Bitterness is allowing the past to hold you back. Think of bitterness as peeling off the scab constantly. Whereas forgiveness is freedom from the past. How can you calculate forgiveness? Jesus said the calculation for forgiveness was 70x7.

When we don't forgive, it's oftentimes because we feel that we have been hurt by others and do not deserve that. But how long you will stay hurt is really up to you. You're the only one that can let it go. If you hold on to hurt, you not only hurt yourself, but you also hurt others. Why? Because hurt people hurt people. So that decision of letting go is entirely yours. You keep reinfecting yourself, every time you nourish bitterness. Jesus said that the forgiveness that you extend to others will be extended to you. Forgiveness will make you more than a conqueror. Because not only will you win the battle over your bitterness, but in forgiving the one who has offended you, you also win a friend.

* **Mt 6:14, 15** For if you forgive men their trespasses, your heavenly Father will also forgive you. But if you do not forgive men their trespasses, neither will your Father forgive your trespasses.

Mk 11:25 And whenever you stand praying, if you have anything against anyone, forgive him, that your Father in heaven may also forgive you your trespasses.

Mt 18:21, 22, 35 Then Peter came to Him and said, "Lord, how often shall my brother sin against me, and I forgive him? Up to seven times?" Jesus said to him, "I do not say to you, up to seven times, but up to seventy times seven. So My heavenly Father also will do to you if each of you, from his heart, does not forgive his brother his trespasses".

Ps 18:25 With the merciful You will show Yourself merciful; with a blameless man You will show Yourself blameless.

Pr 3:3, 4 Let not mercy and truth forsake you; bind them around your neck, write them on the tablet of your heart, and so find favor and high esteem in the sight of God and man.

Pr 10:12 Hatred stirs up strife, but love covers all sins.

Mt 5:7 Blessed are the merciful, for they shall obtain mercy.

* **Mt 7:12** Therefore, whatever you want men to do to you, do also to them, for this is the law and the prophets.

Lk 6:36, 37 Therefore be merciful, just as your Father also is merciful. Judge not, and you shall not be judged. Condemn not, and you shall not be condemned. Forgive, and you will be forgiven.

Lk 7:47 Therefore I say to you, her sins, which are many, are forgiven, for she loved much. But to whom little is forgiven, the same loves little.

Lk 17:4 And if he sins against you seven times in a day, and seven times in a day returns to you, saying, 'I repent,' you shall forgive him.

Ro 12:19-21 Beloved, do not avenge yourselves, but rather give place to wrath; for it is written, "Vengeance is Mine, I will repay," says the Lord. Therefore, if your enemy is hungry, feed him; ff he is thirsty, give him a drink; for in so doing you will heap coals of fire on his head. Do not be overcome by evil, but overcome evil with good.

* **Eph 4:31, 32** Let all bitterness, wrath, anger, clamor, and evil speaking be put away from you, with all malice. And be kind to one another, tenderhearted, forgiving one another, even as God in Christ forgave you.

Heb 12:15 Looking carefully lest anyone fall short of the grace of God; lest any root of bitterness springing up cause trouble, and by this many become defiled.

* **Col 3:13a, 14** Bearing with one another, and forgiving one another. But above all these things put on love, which is the bond of perfection.

Kind Words and Encouragement

We can use the power of our words to bless others. We need to recognize that the words we speak are windows into our souls. We must make sure we speak the right words. *"The words of a man's mouth are as deep waters, and the wellspring of wisdom as a flowing brook" (Pro18:4).* Deep waters won't run dry. So, encouraging words should ever be present in our mouth. When we remember that God so loves people, it is easy to always speak encouraging words.

There's an old saying that goes like this "Sticks and stones may break my bones, but words will never hurt me". But this saying is totally wrong. Words are actually more powerful than sticks and stones and can hurt longer. We need to watch the words we say. We can hurt people with our words. But we can also bless people with words. *"Death and life are in the power of the tongue" (Prov. 18:21)*.

Pr 10:11a The mouth of the righteous is a well of life.

* **Eph 4:29** Let no corrupt word proceed out of your mouth, but what is good for necessary edification, that it may impart grace to the hearers.

Pr 15:1a A soft answer turns away wrath.

Pr 15:4a A wholesome tongue is a tree of life.

Pr 16:1 The preparations of the heart belong to man, but the answer of the tongue is from the Lord.

* **Pr 16:24** Pleasant words are like a honeycomb, sweetness to the soul and health to the bones.

Pr 14:3b The lips of the wise will preserve them.

Pr 31:26b On her tongue is the law of kindness.

2Chr 10:7 And they spoke to him, saying, "If you are kind to these people, and please them, and speak good words to them, they will be your servants forever."

* **Ps 19:14** Let the words of my mouth and the meditation of my heart be acceptable in Your sight, O Lord, my strength and my Redeemer.

* **Ps 35:28** And my tongue shall speak of Your righteousness and of Your praise all the day long.

XIII. POWERFUL PROMISES OF GOD IN TIMES OF DIFFICULTIES

All throughout God's Word, there are many promises given to us for supply, protection, comfort and for our overall well-being. Some are conditional on our obedience, and others are unconditional. The Bible says that none of His good promises will return to Him void. That means that they are bound to bear fruit in our lives, if we stand firm on them.

Below are different sections in which we have listed many of God's promises to refer to in times of stress, worry, persecution, etc., so that we are reminded of His protection, comfort, supply, peace, etc. The key to looking to God's Word and depending on His promises is to make them our own by verbalizing them to ourselves.

Wise is he in the day of trouble who knows his true source of strength and fails not to pray. Prayer ministers strength and comfort in times of trouble and begets patience and endurance to bear it. Rich and poor alike are all partakers of the painful and troublesome inheritance of the fall of man. God does not assume responsibility for the source of trouble, but He is able to work it into His divine purpose to achieve the welfare of His saints. We know that all things work together for good to them that love God and with every temptation He will make a way to escape *(1 Cor 10:13)*.

God doesn't punish us, nor judge us through trouble; all judgment and punishment took place on the cross. The troubles we're facing are not God's dealings with us. However, He'll use our difficulties and tribulations to teach us and to train us. God's dealings with His people is of the nature of training as in "discipling us". Good and bad alike experience trouble. "The rain falls on the just and on the unjust" *(Mt 5:45)*. Therefore trouble is no evidence of God's displeasure, but of the fallen world.

Trouble has no power in itself to interfere with our relationship with God. *"Who shall separate us from the love of God...tribulation, distress, persecutions, famine, peril, sword?" (Rom 8:35).*

God has pardoned our iniquity so there is assuredly no condemnation on the behalf of God. His part is to comfort the brokenhearted. *"I will not leave you comfortless" (Jn 14:18)*. *"Call upon me in the day of trouble and I will deliver you"* (Ps 50:15).

King David was known to inquire of the Lord in times of trouble and before every battle. And there lied his strength and his victories. *"That we may obtain mercy and grace in times of trouble" (Heb 4:16)*.

Prayer delivers us of unbelief, saves us from doubting and drives away foolish and vain questioning. *"In all this, Job sinned not, nor charged God foolishly" (Job 1:20)*. Prayer has the ability to unburden the heart of grief and bring the spirit of man in perfect submission, and cause us to trust God's promises. The good or the evil of trouble is always determined by the spirit in which it is perceived and received. It will either soften or harden the heart. It either draws us to God or from God.

In the New Testament, there are three words employed for trouble; tribulation, suffering, and affliction. The Lord told his disciples to expect tribulation in the world, but to be of good cheer. Paul said we must go through much tribulation in order to enter into the kingdom. *"And I reckon that the sufferings of this present world are not worthy to be compared with the glory that will be revealed in us" (Rom 8:18)*.

And, *"for our light affliction which is but for a moment, brings out a far exceeding and eternal weight of glory" (1Cor 4:15)*. *"Rejoicing in hope, patient and tribulation, continuing instant in prayer" (Rom 12:12)*. Rich spiritual fruits come from tribulation. So suffering and the highest forms of grace are related. *"After you have suffered a while, make you perfect, established, strengthened and settle you" (1 Pt 5:10)*. It is in the furnace of testing that faith turns to patience and then to immovable trust.

Peace that Passes all Understanding

Once you truly understand the love of God for you and the new identity that He has created you into, it gives you so much

XIII. POWERFUL PROMISES OF GOD

peace of heart and mind. All stress is gone. You have entered into the true rest (the Sabbath) of God. And you reflect a peace that passes all understanding.

Phil 4:5, 6 Let your gentleness be known to all men. The Lord is at hand. Be anxious for nothing, but in everything by prayer and supplication, with thanksgiving, let your requests be made known to God.

* **Isa 26:3** You will keep him in perfect peace, whose mind is stayed on You, because he trusts in You.

* **Jn 14:27** Peace I leave with you, My peace I give to you; not as the world gives do I give to you. Let not your heart be troubled, neither let it be afraid.

* **1Jn 4:18** There is no fear in love; but perfect love casts out fear, because fear involves torment. But he who fears has not been made perfect in love.

* **2Tim 1:7** For God has not given us a spirit of fear, but of power and of love and of a sound mind.

  Mt 6:34 Therefore do not worry about tomorrow, for tomorrow will worry about its own things. Sufficient for the day is its own trouble.

  Ps 55:22 Cast your burden on the LORD, and He shall sustain you; He shall never permit the righteous to be moved.

* **Isa 12:2a** God is my salvation, I will trust and not be afraid.

* **Isa 41:10** Fear not, for I am with you; be not dismayed, for I am your God. I will strengthen you, yes, I will help you, I will uphold you with My righteous right hand.

  Isa 41:13 For I, the Lord your God, will hold your right hand, saying to you, 'Fear not, I will help you'.

* **Ps 119:165** Great peace have those who love Your law, and nothing causes them to stumble.

* **Ps 34:4** I sought the Lord, and He heard me, and delivered me from all my fears.

* **Ps 23:4** Yea, though I walk through the valley of the shadow of death, I will fear no evil; for You are with me; Your rod and Your staff, they comfort me.
* **Ps 27:1** The Lord is my light and my salvation; whom shall I fear? The Lord is the strength of my life; of whom shall I be afraid?
* **Ps 46:1, 2** God is our refuge and strength, a very present help in trouble. Therefore will not we fear, though the earth be removed, and though the mountains be carried into the midst of the sea.
* **Ps 56:3, 4** Whenever I am afraid, I will trust in You. In God I will praise His Word, in God I have put my trust; I will not fear. What can flesh do to me?

  Ps 91:2, 5 I will say of the Lord, He is my refuge and my fortress; My God, in Him I will trust. You shall not be afraid of the terror by night, nor of the arrow that flies by day.
* **Pr 1:33** But whoever listens to Me will dwell safely, and will be secure, without fear of evil.

  Pr 3:24-26 When you lie down, you will not be afraid; Yes, you will lie down and your sleep will be sweet. Do not be afraid of sudden terror, nor of trouble from the wicked when it comes; For the Lord will be your confidence, and will keep your foot from being caught.
* **Pr 29:25** The fear of man brings a snare, but whoever trusts in the Lord shall be safe.
* **Jer 1:8** Do not be afraid of their faces, for I am with you to deliver you," says the Lord.
* **Mk 5:36b** Do not be afraid; only believe.
* **Deut 31:6** Be strong and of a good courage, fear not, nor be afraid of them: for the Lord thy God, He it is that doth go with thee; He will not fail thee, nor forsake thee.

XIII. POWERFUL PROMISES OF GOD

Do not Fear

Fear is the opposite of faith. It takes as much energy on our mind to worry or stress about something as it does to meditate on God's promises and focus our thoughts on the possibilities of God. Fear is the enemy's favorite weapon on our mind to cause us not to trust and have faith in God. He knows that faith is the key to appropriate God's promises to us and Satan will do anything to cause us to worry, fear and stress.

Unfortunately, we sometimes put our lives on hold because of fear. Fear can be conquered through renewing our mind with the truth of God's Word. Lies and truth can't coexist. God gives us the power to live courageously, boldly, fearlessly in this life, when many things that surround us would tell us to be afraid.

1Jn 4:18 There is no fear in love; but perfect love casts out fear, because fear involves torment. But he who fears has not been made perfect in love.

Phil 4:6, 7 Be anxious for nothing, but in everything by prayer and supplication, with thanksgiving, let your requests be made known to God; and the peace of God, which surpasses all understanding, will guard your hearts and minds through Christ Jesus.

Ps 94:19 In the multitude of my anxieties within me, Your comforts delight my soul.

Isa 43:1b Fear not, for I have redeemed you; I have called you by your name; you are Mine.

Pr 12:25 Anxiety in the heart of man causes depression, but a good word makes it glad.

Josh 1:9 Have I not commanded you? Be strong and of good courage; do not be afraid, nor be dismayed, for the LORD your God is with you wherever you go.

Isa 35:4 Say to those who are fearful-hearted, "Be strong, do not fear! Behold, your God will come with vengeance, with the recompense of God; He will come and save you."

Isa 41:13 For I, the LORD your God, will hold your right hand, saying to you, 'Fear not, I will help you.'

Ps 118:6 The LORD is on my side; I will not fear. What can man do to me?

Pro 29:25 The fear of man brings a snare, but whoever trusts in the LORD shall be safe.

Mk 4:39, 40 Then He arose and rebuked the wind, and said to the sea, "Peace, be still!" And the wind ceased and there was a great calm. But He said to them, "Why are you so fearful? How is it that you have no faith?"

1Pt 3:14 But even if you should suffer for righteousness' sake, you are blessed. And do not be afraid of their threats, nor be troubled.

Deut 3:22 You must not fear them, for the LORD your God Himself fights for you.

1Chr 28:20b Be strong and of good courage, and do it: fear not, nor be dismayed: for the Lord God, even my God, will be with thee; He will not fail thee, nor forsake thee, until thou hast finished all the work for the service of the house of the Lord.

Zeph 3:17 The LORD your God in your midst, the mighty One, will save; He will rejoice over you with gladness, He will quiet you with His love, He will rejoice over you with singing.

Ps 91:1-16 He who dwells in the secret place of the Most High Shall abide under the shadow of the Almighty. I will say of the Lord, "He is my refuge and my fortress; My God, in Him I will trust." Surely He shall deliver you from the snare of the fowler and from the perilous pestilence. He shall cover you with His feathers, and under His wings you shall take refuge; His truth shall be your shield and buckler. You shall not be afraid of the terror by night, nor of the arrow that flies by day, nor of the pestilence that walks in darkness, nor of the destruction that lays waste at noonday. A thousand may fall at your side, and ten thousand at your right hand; but it shall not come near you. Only with your eyes shall you look and see the reward of the wicked. Because you have made the Lord, who is my refuge, even the Most High, your dwelling place, no evil shall befall you, nor shall any plague come near your dwelling; for He shall give His angels charge over you, to keep you in all your ways. In their hands they shall bear you up, lest you dash your foot against a stone. You shall tread upon the lion and the cobra, the young lion and the serpent you shall trample underfoot. Because he has set his love upon Me, therefore I will deliver him; I will set him on high, because he has known My name. He shall call upon Me, and I will answer him; I will be with him in trouble; I will deliver him and honor him. With long life I will satisfy him, and show him My salvation.

(Please read also "Peace that Passes all Understanding")

Claim God's Protection

God has given us hundreds of promises for His protection. We are not always equal to the task or to the attack, but God will always protect us and deliver us when we look to Him.

Deut 33:12 The beloved of the Lord shall dwell in safety by Him; and the Lord shall cover him all the day long, and he shall dwell between His shoulders.

2Chr 14:11b Lord, it is nothing for You to help, whether with many or with those who have no power; help us, O Lord our God, for we rest on You, and in Your name we go against this multitude. O Lord, You are our God; do not let man prevail against You!

2Chr 20:12 O our God, will You not judge them? For we have no power against this great multitude that is coming against us; nor do we know what to do, but our eyes are upon You.

* **Isa 59:1** Behold, the Lord's hand is not shortened that it cannot save; nor His ear heavy that it cannot hear.

Ps 3:1-3 Lord, how they have increased who trouble me! Many are they who rise up against me. Many are they who say of me, "There is no help for him in God." But You, O Lord, are a shield for me, My glory and the One who lifts up my head.

Ps 5:11a But let all those rejoice who put their trust in You; Let them ever shout for joy, because You defend them.

Ps 9:13, 14 Have mercy on me, O Lord! Consider my trouble from those who hate me, You who lift me up from the gates of death, that I may tell of all Your praise In the gates of the daughter of Zion. I will rejoice in Your salvation.

Ps 7:1 O Lord my God, in You I put my trust; save me from all those who persecute me; and deliver me.

Ps 16:1 Preserve me, O God, for in You I put my trust.

Ps 17:8, 9 Keep me as the apple of Your eye; hide me under the shadow of Your wings from the wicked who oppress me, from my deadly enemies who surround me.

Ps 18:3 I will call upon the Lord, Who is worthy to be praised; so shall I be saved from my enemies.

Ps 18:48 He delivers me from my enemies. You also lift me up above those who rise against me; You have delivered me from the violent man.

Ps 25:1-3 To You, O Lord, I lift up my soul. O my God, I trust in You; let me not be ashamed; let not my enemies triumph over me. Indeed, let no one who waits on You be ashamed; let those be ashamed who deal treacherously without cause.

Ps 27:5 For in the time of trouble He shall hide me in His pavilion; in the secret place of His tabernacle He shall hide me; He shall set me high upon a rock.

Ps 27:12-14 Do not deliver me to the will of my adversaries; for false witnesses have risen against me, and such as breathe out violence. I would have lost heart, unless I had believed that I would see the goodness of the Lord in the land of the living.

XIII. POWERFUL PROMISES OF GOD

Ps 31:1-4 In You, O Lord, I put my trust; let me never be ashamed; deliver me in Your righteousness. Bow down Your ear to me, deliver me speedily; be my rock of refuge, a fortress of defense to save me. For You are my rock and my fortress; Therefore, for Your name's sake, pull me out of the net which they have secretly laid for me, for You are my strength.

Ps 31:18 Let the lying lips be put to silence, which speak insolent things proudly and contemptuously against the righteous.

Ps 31:13, 14a For I hear the slander of many; fear is on every side; while they take counsel together against me, they scheme to take away my life. But as for me, I trust in You, O Lord

Ps 34:17 The righteous cry out, and the Lord hears, and delivers them out of all their troubles.

Ps 35:1 Plead my cause, O Lord, with those who strive with me; fight against those who fight against me.

Ps 50:15 Call upon Me in the day of trouble; I will deliver you, and you shall glorify Me.

Ps 56:9-11 When I cry out to You, then my enemies will turn back; this I know, because God is for me. In God I have put my trust; I will not be afraid. What can man do to me?

Ps 59:16, 17 But I will sing of Your power; yes, I will sing aloud of Your mercy in the morning; for You have been my defense and refuge in the day of my trouble. To You, O my Strength, I will sing praises; for God is my defense, my God of mercy.

Ps 61:2, 4 From the end of the earth I will cry to You. When my heart is overwhelmed; lead me to the rock that is higher than I. I will abide in Your tabernacle forever; I will trust in the shelter of Your wings.

Ps 62:6 He only is my rock and my salvation; He is my defense; I shall not be moved.

Ps 91:4 He shall cover you with His feathers, and under His wings you shall take refuge; His truth shall be your shield and buckler.

Ps 118:6, 7 The Lord is on my side; I will not fear. What can man do to me? The Lord is for me among those who help me; therefore I shall see my desire on those who hate me.

Ps 91:9, 10 Because you have made the Lord, who is my refuge, even the Most High, your dwelling place, no evil shall befall you, nor shall any plague come near your dwelling.

Ps 119:110, 154 The wicked have laid a snare for me, yet I have not strayed from Your precepts. Plead my cause and redeem me; revive me according to Your Word.

Ps 121:8 The Lord shall preserve your going out and your coming in from this time forth, and even forevermore.

* **Ps 127:1b** Unless the Lord guards the city, the watchman stays awake in vain.

Ps 141:8-10 But my eyes are upon You, O God the Lord; in You I take refuge; do not leave my soul destitute. Keep me from the snares they have laid for me, and from the traps of the workers of iniquity. Let the wicked fall into their own nets, while I escape safely.

Ps 143:8, 9 Cause me to hear Your lovingkindness in the morning, for in You do I trust; cause me to know the way in which I should walk, for I lift up my soul to You. Deliver me, O Lord, from my enemies. In You I take shelter.

* **Lk 10:19** I give you the authority to trample on serpents and scorpions, and over all the power of the enemy, and nothing shall by any means hurt you.

Ps 144:1, 2a Blessed be the Lord my Rock, who trains my hands for war, and my fingers for battle. My lovingkindness and my fortress. My high tower and my deliverer. My shield and the One in whom I take refuge.

Ps 145:18-20a The Lord is near to all who call upon Him, to all who call upon Him in truth. He will fulfill the desire of those who fear Him; He also will hear their cry and save them. The Lord preserves all who love Him.

* **Pr 14:26** In the fear of the Lord there is strong confidence, and His children will have a place of refuge.
* **Pr 18:10** The name of the Lord is a strong tower; the righteous run to it and are safe.

Isa 35:3, 4 Strengthen the weak hands, and make firm the feeble knees. Say to those who are fearful-hearted, "Be strong, do not fear! Behold, your God will come with vengeance, with the recompense of God; He will come and save you."

Isa 43:2 When you pass through the waters, I will be with you; and through the rivers, they shall not overflow you. When you walk through the fire, you shall not be burned, nor shall the flame scorch you.

Isa 50:7 For the Lord God will help Me; therefore, I will not be disgraced; therefore, I have set My face like a flint, and I know that I will not be ashamed.

2Cor 4:8, 9 We are hard-pressed on every side, yet not crushed; we are perplexed, but not in despair; persecuted, but not forsaken; struck down, but not destroyed.

1Pt 3:12, 13 For the eyes of the Lord are on the righteous, and His ears are open to their prayers; but the face of the Lord is against those who do evil. And who is he who will harm you if you become followers of what is good?

* **Exo 14:14** The Lord will fight for you, and you shall hold your peace.
* **Ps 34:7** The angel of the LORD encamps all around those who fear Him, and delivers them.

Depend on His Strength and Power

Our strength is in God. To say that we can do anything on our own is depending on "the arm of the flesh". All those who acknowledged God before battles were blessed of God, but those who moved in their own strength lost the battle.

* **2Cor 12:9, 10** And He said to me, "My grace is sufficient for you, for My strength is made perfect in weakness." Therefore most gladly I will rather boast in my infirmities, that the power of Christ may rest upon me. Therefore I take pleasure in infirmities, in reproaches, in needs, in persecutions, in distresses, for Christ's sake. For when I am weak, then I am strong.
* **Zech 4:6b** Not by might nor by power, but by My Spirit, says the Lord of hosts.

   Deut 20:4 For the Lord your God is He who goes with you, to fight for you against your enemies, to save you.

   2Chr 32:8a With him is an arm of flesh; but with us is the Lord our God, to help us and to fight our battles.
* **Neh 8:10b** The joy of the Lord is your strength.
* **Isa 30:15b** In quietness and confidence shall be your strength.

   Isa 40:29-31 He gives power to the weak, and to those who have no might He increases strength. Even the youths shall faint and be weary, and the young men shall utterly fall, but those who wait on the Lord shall renew their strength; They shall mount up with wings like eagles, they shall run and not be weary, they shall walk and not faint.
* **Jer 32:27** Behold, I am the Lord, the God of all flesh. Is there anything too hard for Me?

   Ps 18:29, 30b, 32 For by You I can run against a troop, by my God I can leap over a wall. He is a shield to all who trust in Him. It is God who arms me with strength, and makes my way perfect.

   Ps 20:7 Some trust in chariots, and some in horses; but we will remember the name of the Lord our God.

   Ps 27:13, 14 I would have lost heart, unless I had believed that I would see the goodness of the Lord in the land of the living. Wait on the Lord; be of good courage, and He shall strengthen your heart; wait, I say, on the Lord!

XIII. POWERFUL PROMISES OF GOD

Ps 28:7, 8 The Lord is my strength and my shield; my heart trusted in Him, and I am helped; therefore my heart greatly rejoices, and with my song I will praise Him. The Lord is their strength, and He is the saving refuge of His anointed.

Ps 37:39 But the salvation of the righteous is from the Lord; He is their strength in the time of trouble.

Ps 60:11 Give us help from trouble, for the help of man is useless.

Ps 73:26 My flesh and my heart fail; but God is the strength of my heart and my portion forever.

Ps 84:5, 7a Blessed is the man whose strength is in You, whose heart is set on pilgrimage. They go from strength to strength.

* **Ps 118:8** It is better to trust in the Lord than to put confidence in man.

Ps 118:14 The Lord is my strength and song, and He has become my salvation.

Ps 119:28 My soul melts from heaviness; strengthen me according to Your Word.

2Cor 3:5 Not that we are sufficient of ourselves to think of anything as being from ourselves, but our sufficiency is from God.

* **Eph 6:10-12** Finally, my brethren, be strong in the Lord and in the power of His might. Put on the whole armor of God that you may be able to stand against the wiles of the devil. For we do not wrestle against flesh and blood, but against principalities, against powers, against the rulers of the darkness of this age, against spiritual hosts of wickedness in the heavenly places.

* **Phil 4:13** I can do all things through Christ who strengthens me.

* **Mt 10:20** For it is not you who speak, but the Spirit of your Father who speaks in you.

* **Phil 2:13** For it is God who works in you both to will and to do for His good pleasure.

* **Jer 17:5** Thus says the Lord: 'Cursed is the man who trusts in man and makes flesh his strength, whose heart departs from the Lord.'
* **2Cor 4:7** But we have this treasure in earthen vessels, that the excellence of the power may be of God and not of us.
* **Isa 40:31** But those who wait on the Lord shall renew their strength; they shall mount up with wings like eagles, they shall run and not be weary, they shall walk and not faint.
* **Deut 33:25b** As your days, so shall your strength be.
* **Acts 4:13** Now when they saw the boldness of Peter and John, and perceived that they were uneducated and untrained men, they marveled and they realized that they had been with Jesus.

God Promises Comfort in Tribulation

We have so many promises in God's Word for an abundantly, blessed life. But there are times when we face real difficulties, afflictions, tragedies and tribulations. And even during those challenging times, God has promised help and strength, grace and mercy to get us through. We must hold tight to His promises when life is difficult! He is the God of possibilities and solutions and He has promised us deliverance and comfort in every situation.

* **2Cor 1:4** Who comforts us in all our tribulation, that we may be able to comfort those who are in any trouble, with the comfort with which we ourselves are comforted by God.
* **Ps 119:50** This is my comfort in my affliction, for Your Word has given me life.

   Ps 71:21 You shall increase my greatness, and comfort me on every side.

   Ps 34:18 The Lord is near to those who have a broken heart, and saves such as have a contrite spirit.

   Ps 37:24 Though he fall, he shall not be utterly cast down; for the Lord upholds him with His hand..

Ps 55:22 Cast your burden on the Lord, and He shall sustain you; He shall never permit the righteous to be moved.

Ps 112:4 Unto the upright there arises light in the darkness; He is gracious, and full of compassion, and righteous.

Ps 145:14 The Lord upholds all who fall, and raises up all who are bowed down.

* **Ps 147:3** He heals the brokenhearted and binds up their wounds.
* **Mt 5:4** Blessed are those who mourn, for they shall be comforted.

Jn 14:16-18 And I will pray the Father, and He will give you another Helper, that He may abide with you forever— the Spirit of truth, whom the world cannot receive, because it neither sees Him nor knows Him; but you know Him, for He dwells with you and will be in you. I will not leave you orphans; I will come to you.

* **Heb 13:5b** For He Himself has said, "I will never leave you nor forsake you."

2Cor 1:7 And our hope for you is steadfast, because we know that as you are partakers of the sufferings, so also you will partake of the consolation.

2Cor 7:4b I am filled with comfort. I am exceedingly joyful in all our tribulation.

2Thes 2:16, 17 Now may our Lord Jesus Christ Himself, and our God and Father, who has loved us and given us everlasting consolation and good hope by grace, comfort your hearts and establish you in every good word and work.

Get His Wisdom and Knowledge

The knowledge that God gives us is rooted in His Word and it gives us wisdom to know how to handle situations. When we need counsel, guidance, advice and answers, there is more information available to us now than has ever been, at our fingertips and instantly! However, for the greatest wisdom in seeking the right information, use God's Word as your guide. There is every answer known to man in the instructions that God has given. It is so important for Christians to know God's Word in order to give an answer to him that asks any question.

Pr 2:6 For the LORD gives wisdom; from His mouth come knowledge and understanding.

Pr 1:7 The fear of the LORD is the beginning of knowledge, but fools despise wisdom and instruction.

Pr 18:15 The heart of the prudent acquires knowledge, and the ear of the wise seeks knowledge.

Pr 15:14 The heart of him who has understanding seeks knowledge, but the mouth of fools feeds on foolishness.

Pr 11:14 Where there is no guidance the people fall, but in abundance of counselors there is victory.

Pr 12:15 The way of a fool is right in his own eyes, but a wise man is he who listens to counsel.

Pr 19:20, 21 Listen to counsel and accept discipline that you may be wise the rest of your days. Many plans are in a man's heart, but the counsel of the Lord will stand.

Pr 28:26 He who trusts in his own heart is a fool, but he who walks wisely will be delivered.

Pr 20:18 Plans are established by counsel; by wise counsel wage war.

Pr 4:13 Take hold of instruction; do not let go. Guard her, for she is your life.

Pr 2:1, 2 My son, if you receive my words and treasure my commands within you, so that you incline your ear to wisdom, and apply your heart to understanding.

Ps 119:66 Teach me good judgment and knowledge, for I believe Your commandments.

Isa 11:2 The Spirit of the LORD shall rest upon Him, the Spirit of wisdom and understanding, the Spirit of counsel and might, the Spirit of knowledge and of the fear of the LORD.

Pr 20:15 There is gold and a multitude of rubies, but the lips of knowledge are a precious jewel.

XIV. CREATION VS. EVOLUTION

Creation speaks of the glories of God's love and His power! Everything we see around us holds the wonders of a great and magnificent God of love!

Most people today have been so deceived into believing that the theory of evolution is true, that it never even occurs to them to question or doubt it! The Bible warns us to *"avoid the profane and vain babblings and oppositions of science falsely so called!" (1Tim 6:20)*.

The world has become so deceived, that Evolution is now referred to in most textbooks as "fact". But there is no proof for the theory of evolution! Therefore it must be believed by faith like any religion.

At the core of evolutionary theory is the big assumption that life somehow arose from non-life by pure blind chance, that there simply happened to be the right chemicals in the right place, in the right arrangement, it was just the right time and conditions, and then suddenly - Presto! Some unknown electro-chemical process took place and life created itself! It takes more faith to believe evolution, this incredible, fictitious, confused, self-contradicting fairy tale of man's origins than it does to accept God's simple, inspired explanation in His Word.

Margaret Mead, the famed evolutionist, said in the introduction to her book, "We as honest scientists must confess that there is not <u>one</u> iota of concrete <u>evidence</u> to support the theory of evolution." So evolution is merely a set of beliefs that must be accepted by faith. It is literally a religion invented by the devil to deter people from believing in God!

The same as a building requires a builder, an absolutely mind-boggling heaven, earth and all living creation requires a creator! When we take the time to look into the intricacies of even the tiniest creature, or the DNA of human life, or stand in awe at the power of a storm, we will be compelled to say as the Psalmist David, *"The heavens declare the glory of God, and the firmament shows His handiwork"*, and *"I will praise Him, for I am fearfully and wonderfully made" (Ps 19:1 and Ps 139:14)*.

XIV. CREATION VS. EVOLUTION

Gen 1:1, 11, 12 In the beginning God created the heavens and the earth. Then God said, "Let the earth bring forth grass, the herb that yields seed, and the fruit tree that yields fruit according to its kind, whose seed is in itself, on the earth"; and it was so. And the earth brought forth grass, the herb that yields seed according to its kind, and the tree that yields fruit, whose seed is in itself according to its kind. And God saw that it was good.

Neh 9:6 You alone are the Lord; You have made heaven, the heaven of heavens, with all their host, the earth and everything on it, the seas and all that is in them, and You preserve them all.

Job 12:7-9 But now ask the beasts, and they will teach you; and the birds of the air, and they will tell you; or speak to the earth, and it will teach you; and the fish of the sea will explain to you. Who among all these does not know that the hand of the Lord has done this.

Job 36:27, 28 For He draws up drops of water, which distill as rain from the mist, which the clouds drop down and pour abundantly on man.

Job 38:22 Have you entered the treasury of snow, or have you seen the treasury of hail.

Ps 14:1 The fool has said in his heart, "There is no God." They are corrupt, they have done abominable works. There is none who does good.

Ps 19:1 The heavens declare the glory of God; and the firmament shows His handiwork.

Is 44:24 Thus says the Lord, your Redeemer, and He who formed you from the womb: "I am the Lord, who makes all things, who stretches out the heavens all alone, who spreads abroad the earth by Myself.

Isa 45:12 I have made the earth, and created man on it. My hands stretched out the heavens and all their host I have commanded.

Jer 10:12, 13 He has made the earth by His power, He has established the world by His wisdom, and has stretched out the heavens at His discretion. When He utters His voice, there is a multitude of waters in the heavens. And He causes the vapors to ascend from the ends of the earth. He makes lightning for the rain, He brings the wind out of His treasuries.

Jn 1:1-3 In the beginning was the Word, and the Word was with God, and the Word was God. He was in the beginning with God. All things were made through Him, and without Him nothing was made that was made.

Ro 1:20-23 For since the creation of the world His invisible attributes are clearly seen, being understood by the things that are made, even His eternal power and Godhead, so that they are without excuse, because, although they knew God, they did not glorify Him as God, nor were thankful, but became futile in their thoughts, and their foolish hearts were darkened. Professing to be wise, they became fools, and changed the glory of the incorruptible God into an image made like corruptible man—and birds and four-footed animals and creeping things.

Col 1:16 For by Him all things were created that are in heaven and that are on earth, visible and invisible, whether thrones or dominions or principalities or powers. All things were created through Him and for Him.

1Tim 6:20 Timothy! Guard what was committed to your trust, avoiding the profane and idle babblings and contradictions of what is falsely called knowledge.

2Tim 3:7 Always learning and never able to come to the knowledge of the truth.

Heb 1:2 Has in these last days spoken to us by His Son, whom He has appointed heir of all things, through whom also He made the worlds;

Heb 1:3 Who being the brightness of His glory and the express image of His person, and upholding all things by the word of His power, when He had by Himself purged our sins, sat down at the right hand of the Majesty on high.

XIV. CREATION VS. EVOLUTION

Heb 11:3 By faith we understand that the worlds were framed by the Word of God, so that the things which are seen were not made of things which are visible.

XV. THE END OF TIME

The subject of the "end time" is known to Christians and non-Christians alike as a period of time, specifically and prophetically spoken of in the Old and New Testaments. There are controversial and differing doctrines concerning this period of time, but <u>all agree that this period will certainly take place</u>.

People have asked, "What can we do to prepare for the endtime events?" Exercising your faith daily by serving the Lord is definitely a must as we can't expect our faith to be all muscled-up if we have not been living for God all along. We have to keep our faith muscles in shape. We can't be a "couch potato" spiritually, and expect to have faith instantly when we need it. It doesn't work that way.

Our prayer habits are also very important to keep up, as well as to be able to hear from the Lord. Regular Word time is another must; when you read the Word you will be stronger. It's like the immune system in your body. You need a daily diet of Word time & this includes memorizing & having the Word deep in your being, soul & spirit. And cultivate an intimate relationship with the Lord: this takes time, effort and consistency. It doesn't come overnight.

Also, spend your time in ways that are meaningful & that will build yourself up to increase & add value to your life. For example, taking a course in First Aid can be done even online, or a course on growing a garden rather than binging on movies. You may want to have Bible classes on endtime events together with others and study as a group, research & discuss together. This will help the Word to have greater impact, deeper effect & remember it better & be able to apply & process it more intentionally.

Lastly, manage your time wisely & schedule your priorities. Dump time-wasters & things not beneficial to helping you be a better Christian.

Below, we have given a detailed outline of these prophetic end time events. We have included what are the most important verses as highlighted by Jesus as "the signs of the end". (See

Matthew 24) If you'd like to do an in depth study on the time of the end, go through all these verses to fully understand these amazing events that are to come.

The Signs of the Endtime

Knowledge shall be Increased

Dan 12:4 But you, Daniel, shut up the words, and seal the book until the time of the end; many shall run to and fro, and knowledge shall increase.

* **2Tim 3:1, 7** But know this, that in the last days perilous times will come: always learning and never able to come to the knowledge of the truth.

Mt 24:14 And this gospel of the kingdom will be preached in all the world as a witness to all the nations, and then the end will come.

Greatly Increased Natural Disasters

Mt 24:7 For nation will rise against nation, and kingdom against kingdom. And there will be famines, pestilences, and earthquakes in various places.

Lk 21:26 Men's hearts failing them from fear and the expectation of those things which are coming on the earth, for the powers of the heavens will be shaken.

Greatly Increased Wickedness and Wars

2Tim 3:1, 13 But know this, that in the last days perilous times will come: But evil men and impostors will grow worse and worse, deceiving and being deceived.

Mt 24:6 And you will hear of wars and rumors of wars. See that you are not troubled; for all these things must come to pass, but the end is not yet.

Mt 24:37, 38 But as the days of Noah were, so also will the coming of the Son of Man be. For as in the days before the flood, they were eating and drinking, marrying and giving in marriage, until the day that Noah entered the ark.

Lk 21:25 And there will be signs in the sun, in the moon, and in the stars; and on the earth distress of nations, with perplexity, the sea and the waves roaring.

Rampant Perversion in the Endtime

Lk 17:28-30 Likewise as it was also in the days of Lot: they ate, they drank, they bought, they sold, they planted, they built; but on the day that Lot went out of Sodom it rained fire and brimstone from heaven and destroyed them all. Even so will it be in the day when the Son of Man is revealed.

Ro 1:24 Therefore God also gave them up to uncleanness, in the lusts of their hearts, to dishonor their bodies among themselves.

2Tim 3:1-3 But know this, that in the last days perilous times will come: for men will be lovers of themselves, lovers of money, boasters, proud, blasphemers, disobedient to parents, unthankful, unholy, unloving, unforgiving, slanderers, without self-control, brutal, despisers of good.

* **Hos 3:5** Afterward the children of Israel shall return and seek the Lord their God and David their king. They shall fear the Lord and His goodness in the latter days.

Great Falling away from True Faith

2Thes 2:2, 3 Not to be soon shaken in mind or troubled, either by spirit or by word or by letter, as if from us, as though the day of Christ had come. Let no one deceive you by any means; for that day will not come unless the falling away comes first, and the man of sin is revealed, the son of perdition.

Mt 24:12 And because lawlessness will abound, the love of many will grow cold.

Mt 24:5, 11, 24 For many will come in My name, saying, 'I am the Christ,' and will deceive many. Then many false prophets will rise up and deceive many. For false christs and false

XV. THE END OF TIME

prophets will rise and show great signs and wonders to deceive, if possible, even the elect.

1Tim 4:1 Now the Spirit expressly says that in latter times some will depart from the faith, giving heed to deceiving spirits and doctrines of demons.

Increased Persecution of True Christians

Mt 24:9, 10 Then they will deliver you up to tribulation and kill you, and you will be hated by all nations for My name's sake. And then many will be offended, will betray one another, and will hate one another.

Lk 21:16, 17 You will be betrayed even by parents and brothers, relatives and friends; and they will put some of you to death. And you will be hated by all for My name's sake.

The Antichrist

How to Recognise the Antichrist World Government: Dan.8:25; Dan.11:21; Dan.11:23-24; Dan.11:39b; Dan.11:36,37

The Rise of the Antichrist: 1Jn.2:18; 2Thes.2:1-4; 2Thes.2:9; 2Thes.2:10-12; Dan.8:23; Rev.13:4; Rev.13:7; Dan.11:37

Signing of the Covenant: Dan.9:27a; Dan.11:30b-3

Breaking of the Covenant/Daily Sacrifice (Jewish Worship) Stopped: Dan.8:11, 12; Dan.9:27b; Dan.11:31; 2Thes.2:4

Great Tribulation

A Time of Intense Trouble and Persecution: Dan.12:1b; Mat.24:15, 21; Mat.24:22

Antichrist Blasphemes, Says He Is God: Dan.7:25a; 2Thes.2:3b, 4; Rev.13:6

Much of the World Worships Him: Rev. 13:3b-4 Rev.13:8; Rev.13:13, 14

The Mark, the Image and Enforced Worship of the Beast: Rev.13:15; Rev.13:16, 17; Rev.13:18; Rev.14:9-11

The False Prophet
Rev.13:11-16; Rev.19:20

The Antichrist's Persecution of Christians: Rev.13:7; Dan.7:21; Dan.7:25; Dan.8:24; Dan.11:33; Dan.11:35; Dan.12:7b

Why God Allows Us to Suffer Tribulation: Dan.11:35; Dan.12:10; Isa.48:1

Future Heavenly Reward for Enduring Tribulation: Rev.7:9, 13-17; Rev.20:4

Christians Overcome and Survive Despite Persecution: Rev.12:11; Dan.11:32b; Rom.8:35-37; 1Cor.15:51, 52; 1Thes.4:16,1

Protection and Provision during Tribulation: Rev.9:3, 4; Rev.11:3, 5-7; Rev.12:6; Rev.12:14

Witnessing during the Tribulation: Dan.11:33a

Length of the Great Tribulation: Dan.7:25; 1 2:7; Rev.12:14; Rev.11:2; 13:5; Rev.11:3; 12:6

The Second Coming of Jesus Christ
After the Great Tribulation (But before the Wrath): Mat.24:29-30; 2Thes.2:1-3

Jesus' Coming will not be A Secret Event: 1Thes.5:1-4; Mat.24:38, 39; Mat.24:23-26; Mat.24:30; Acts 1:9-11; Rev.1:7

The Tremendous Signs of His Coming: Mat.24:27; Mat.24:29; 1Thes.4:161:7

The Resurrection and Rapture
The Living Raptured, the Dead Resurrected:

1 Thes.4:14; Isa.26:19; 1Thes.4:15, 16; 1 Thes.4:17; Mat.24:31; 1Cor.15:51; 1Cor.15:52; Job 19:25-27; Rev.20:6a; 1Cor.15:53, 54; 2Cor.5:1-4)

Our Powerful, Immortal Resurrection Bodies:

Lk.20:36; Phi.3:20, 21; 1Jn.3:2; Lk.24:36-40; Jn.20:19, 26; Lk.24:30, 31; Lk.24:42,43; Acts 10:40,41; 1Cor.6:14;

1Cor.15:19-55

The Marriage Supper of the Lamb
Dan. 12:2-3; Rev.7:9, 13-17; Rev.19:1, 6-9; Rom.7:4; Hos.2:19, 20; 2Cor. 5:10; 2Cor.11:2

The Judgement Seat of Christ

Christians Rewarded or Punished for Their Works: Rom.14:10-12; 2Cor.5:10; Rev.22:12

Jesus Praises and Rewards Some...Is Ashamed of Others: Dan.12:3; Mat.25:21; 1Cor.3:11-14; 1Cor.3:15; Mk.8:38; Dan.12:2

The Crown of Life ~ a Reward for Faithful Service: Rev.2:10b; Jam.1:12; 2 Tim.4:7, 8

The Wrath of God upon the Earth
God's Wrath upon the Remaining Unsaved: Isa.26:19-21; Isa.13:9-11; Rev.14:9, 10; Rev.16:1-21
The Utter Destruction of Babylon by Fire: Rev.17:1, 5, 18; Rev.18:2, 3, 11; Rev.18:8; Rev.18:17; Rev.17:16

The Battle of Armageddon
The Antichrist, His Allies and Eastern Kings Gather to Fight: Rev.16:12; Rev.16:13, 14; Rev.16:16; Rev.19:19; Ezk.38:1-9

The Lord and His Armies Destroy the Antichrist's Forces: Deut.32:41-43; 2 Thes.1:7-9; Jude 14, 15; Rev.19:11; Rev.19:14, 15; Rev.19:19, 21; Isa.11:4; Rev.19:20

The Cleanup after the Battle: Isa.66:15, 16; Rev.19:17, 18; Ezk.39:17-20; Ezk.39:11, 12

The Millennium

One Thousand Years of Peace: Rev.20:1-3

The Saints Rule with Jesus over all the Earth: Dan.2:44; Dan.7:13,14; Dan.7:18,22,27; Rev.20:4,6; Rev.2:26; Rev.2:27;

Rev.5:10; 2Tim.2:12a; 1Cor.6:2 ; 15:24,25 ; Psa.22:27,28 ; 47:2,3,7,8 ; 72:6-8,11,19

His Rule will be Just and Righteous: Ps 67:4; Psa.72:3, 4; Psa.98:8, 9; Psa. 45:6; Isa.14:5, 7

Heavenly Conditions of the Millennium: Isa.11:6-8; Isa.11:9; Isa.65:25; Hos.2:18

Men will Live for Centuries, like before the Flood: Isa.65:20

Peace on Earth: Isa.14:5-7; Isa.2:4; Ps 46:9

Everyone on Earth will know about the Lord: Isa.2:2, 3; Jer.31:34; Hab.2:14; Psa.22:27

Some will Disobey and be Punished: Zech.14:16, 17; Psa.2:8-10; Isa.26:10

The Battle of Gog and Magog
Ps.2:1-5; Rev.20:7; Rev.20:8,9a; Rev.20:9b; 2Pet.3:10-13; Psa.78:69b; Isa.40:4
Great White Throne Judgement: Rev.20:10; Rev.20:11; Jn.5:29; Rev.20:5a; Rev.20:12, 13; Lk.12:47, 48; Job 34:10, 11; Rev.20:15, 21:8

New Heaven and New Earth
The Heavenly City comes down to Earth: Rev.21:1; Rev.21:10; Rev.21:2; Rev.21:3

Description of the Heavenly City: Heb.11:10; Rev.21:16; Rev.21:12, 17; Rev.21:14, 18-20; Rev.21:12, 21; Rev.21:18; Rev.21:21b; Rev.21:23, 25; Rev.22:1; Rev.22:2; Jn.14:2-3

Only Saved Live in the City; Unsaved Nations Outside: Rev.21:24, 27; Rev.22:2; Heb.11:13-16

Eternal Life and Happiness in Heaven Forever: Rev.21:5; Rev.22:3a; Rev.7:17; Rev.21:4; Rev.21:7; Psa.36:7-9; Heb.13:14

XVI. MEMORY VERSES

What is the New Testament?

Eternally Saved through ONE Sacrifice: Jesus

*Jn 3:16	*Jn 10:27-28	*Jn 6:37
*Jn 14:6	*Acts 4:12	*Ro 3:23
*Jn 3:3b	*Mt 18:3	*Jn 3:36
*Jn 1:12	*Act 16:31	

Grace Replaces the Old Law

*Eph 2:8-9	*Tit 3:5	*Ro 8:2
*Ro 6:23	*Gal 3:13a	*Jn 1:17

Being Born Again

*2Cor 5:17	*Ro 10:9-10	*1Pt 2:2

God's Gift to New Believers: The Holy Spirit

The Spirit of Truth and the Power of God

*Lk 11:13	*Acts 4:31
*Acts 1:8	*Gal 5:22
*Jn 14:26	*Acts 2:17-18
*Jn 16:13	

Hearing from God

*Amos 3:7	*Isa 30:21	*Jer 23:28
*Ps 32:8	*Pr 1:23b	*Ps 73:24a

*Isa 42:9   *Jer 1:9b

The Living Word of God

Jesus is the Word of God – The Creator

*Jn 1:14	*2Tim 2:15	*Jn 15:3
*Mt 4:4	*Jn 6:63	*2Pt 1:4
*Ps 119:11	*Mt 24:35	*Josh 1:8
*Ps 119:130	*1Pt 2:2	*Heb 4:12
*Ps 119:105	*Ps 37:31	

Obedience is the Key~ Faith without Works is Dead

*Jam 1:22-25	*Jn 15:14	*Jam 4:17
*Jn 13:17	*1Sam 15:22-23a	*Jn 14:15

Living a Vibrant Relationship with God is the New Testament

*1Jn 4:19	*2Tim 1:12b	*Ps 111:10a
*Jam 4:8a	*Ro 8:38-39	*Ps 73:25-26
*Pr 8:17	*Ro 7:4	*Rev 3:20
*Mt 11:28-30	*Jn 14:23	

Faith, the only way to Please God

*Ro 10:17	*Jam 1:6-8	*2Tim 2:13
*Pr 3:5-6	*Heb 11:6	*1Jn 5:4
*2Cor 5:7	*Jam 2:26	*Ro 4:20-21
*Mt 9:29b	*Job 13:15a	*Heb 10:35

*Heb 11:1   *Ro 14:23b

Believers are given the Full Authority of Christ

*Mk 9:23
*Lk 1:37

PRAYER: The Believer's Direct Line to God

*Mt 7:7-8	*Jer 33:3	*Mt 18:18
*Jn 15:7	*Mt 18:19-20	*1Jn 5:14-15
*Mk 11:24	*1Jn 3:22	*Isa 45:11b
*Jn 14:14	*1Thes 5:16-18	*Ps 66:18-19
*Jer 29:13	*Heb 4:16	*Ro 8:26
*Isa 65:24		

Praising and Worshiping God

*Eph 5:19-20	*Eph 3:20	*Ps 35:28
*Ps 34:1	*Ps 107:8	*Phil 4:6,8

Discipleship Means "Walking Out" Your Faith

What it Means to be a Christian Disciple

*Lk 14:33	*Mt.6:24	*Mt 9:37-38
*Mt 19:29	*Jn 13:35	*1Cor 6:20
*Lk 9:23-24	*Jn 8:31b-32	*Mt 10: 36-38
*Mt 22:14	*Jn 15:16	*Lk 9:62
*1Cor 11:1	*Mt 23:11	*Pr 11:14

*Heb 13:17   *Pr 27:23

The Christian's Relationship to the World

*Jam 4:4	*Mk 8:36-38	*Eph 5:11
*Jn 15:19	*Gal 5:1	*Ro 12:2
*2Tim 2:4	*2Cor 6:14	*Mt 10:16
*1Jn 2:15	*2Cor 6:17	

Raising Children is "Discipling"

*Heb 12:6, 11	*Pr 22:15	*Ecc 8:11
*Pr 15:32	*Pr 16:6	*Jn 10:11b
*Ps 127:3-5a	*Col 3:20	*Isa 54:13
*Pr 22:6	*1Tim 4:12	

A Surrendered Life (Not My Will)

*Jn 3:30   *Lk 22:42
*Ro 12:1-2   *Ro 6:13a

Christians must Bear Fruit

*Jn 15:4-5	*Ps 1:3	*Heb 11:15-16
*Mt 7:18, 20	*Jn 12:24	*Jn 15:8

Winning the Spiritual Warfare

How to be "More than Conquerors"

*Jam 4:7	*Eph.4:27	*Eph 6:16
*1Jn 4:4	*2Cor 10:4-5	*2Tim 4:18

XVI. MEMORY VERSES

*Isa 59:19b   *1Jn 3:8b
*1Tim 6:12   *1Jn 2:14b

Be "On Guard"

*1Cor 10:13	*Jam 1:12	*2Tim 2:3
*Jam 1:2-3	*Jn 15:2	*Lk 22:31b-32
*Isa 43:1b-2	*Ps 119:67	*1Pt 5:8
*Heb 12:1-2	*Ps 119:71	*Eph 6:10-12
*1Pt 4:12-13	*Heb 5:8	*Ro 8:18
*1Pt 1:7	*Mt 26:41	

Freely You have Received, Freely Give

YOU can be Healed Too!

*Ps 34:19	*Mal 4:2a	*Exo.15:26
*Jam 5:14-15	*Acts 9:34a	*1Jn 1:9
*Isa 40:29	*Ps 107:20	*Isa 53:5
*Ps 103:3	*2Kg 20:5b	
*Lk 17:14b	*Jer 30:17a	

Authority to Heal the Sick, Cast out Demons, Raise the Dead, Cleanse the Lepers

*Mt 10:1
*Mk 16:17-18

Religiosity vs Christianity

Persecution for Christ's Sake

*2Tim 3:12   *Mt 10:23a   *Jn 16:2

*Mt 5:10-12 *Lk 21:17-19 *Acts 5:38b-39
*Ro 8:31b *Jn 15:20 *Mt 5:44
*Lk 21:15 *Phil 1:29

Witnessing Your Faith

The Christian's Love for the World

*1Cor 13:13 *1Jn 4:7-8 *1Cor 16:14
*1Pt 4:8 *Mt 25:40b *Gal 6:2
*1Jn 3:16,18 *1Cor 13:4-8a *Ro 13:8
*Mt 22:37-40 *Jn 15:13 *Mt 7:12
*Jn 13:34 *Gal 5:14

The Great Commission

*Mk.16:15-18 *Pr 11:30 *2Tim 4:2a
*Mt 4:19 *Dan 12:3 *1Cor 2:4-5
*Acts 5:42 *Mt 28:19-20 *1Pt 3:15b
*Mt 5:14-15 *Lk 9:2 *Eze 3:17-19
*1Cor 9:16 *Jn 6:27 *2Tim 2:2

Unity amongst Believers

*Ps 133:1 *Ecc 4:9-10, 12 *Ro 14:19
*Acts 2:44-45 *Eph 4:3 *1Jn 1:7a
*1Cor 1:10 *Ro 12:5

XVI. MEMORY VERSES

Pride

*1Pt 5:5-7	*Pr 16:18	*Pr 11:2
*Phil 2:3	*Dan 4:37b	*Eph 6:6
*Mt 23:12a	*2Cor 10:17	

Finances of the Kingdom

Promises of Blessings

*Phil 4:19	*Ps 84:11b	*Mal 3:10
*Mt 6:33	*Jam 4:2b-3	*Ps 23:1
*Ps 37:3	*1Cor 9:14	*Mt 6:25-2

Stewardship and Integrity

*Rev 2:10	*Lk 16:10	*Eph 5:16
*Mt 25:23	*1Cor 4:2	*Pr 28:20a
*Rev 3:11b	*Ro 12:11	*Gal 6:9

Giving

*Acts 20:35b	*Pr 3:27	*Pr 19:17
*Mt 10:8b	*Lk 6:38	*Ps 41:1
*Mt 5:42	*2Cor 9:6-7	*1Jn 3:17-18

The Power of Our Words

*Ps 19:14   *Eph 4:29   *Pr 29:11
*Mt 12:36-37   *2Tim 2:16   *Pr 16:24
*Mt 12:34b   *Jam 1:19

Bitterness vs Forgiveness

*Eph 4:31-32   *Col 3:13a-14   *Mt 6:14-15

Powerful Promises of God in Times of Difficulties

Depend on His Strength and Power

*Acts 4:13   *Phil 2:13   *Ps 127:1b
*Mt 10:20   *Jer 32:27   *Jer 17:5
*Phil 4:13   *Ps 118:8   *2Cor.4:7
*Neh 8:10b   *Zech 4:6b   Isa 40:31
*Isa 30:15b   *2Cor 12:9-10   *Deut 33:25b

Claim God's Protection

*Lk 10:19   *Exo 14:14   *Ps 34:17
*Isa 59:1   *Ps 34:7   *Pr 18:10
*Pr 14:26

Peace that Passes all Understanding

*Isa 41:10	*1Jn 4:18	*Ps 56:3-4
*Isa 26:3	*Ps 34:4	*Deut 31:6
*2Tim 1:7	*Ps 46:1-2	*Pr 29:25
*Jn 14:27	*Mk 5:36b	*Pr 1:33
*Ps 27:1	*Isa 12:2a	*Ps 119:165
*Ps 23:4	*Jer 1:8	

God Promises Comfort in Tribulation

*2Cor 1:4	*Ps 147:3	*Heb 13:5b
*Ps 119:50	*Jn 14:16-18	*Mt 5:4

Other Special Verses

*Ro 8:28	*Eze 34:23	*Gen 1:1
*Josh 23:14b	*2Chr 20:20b	*Pro 28:13
*1Cor 3:16	*Acts 7:48a	*2Cor 3:17

The End of Time Verses the Last Days

Hos 3:5	2Tim 3:1, 7	1Jn 2:18

Chapters and Passages

(To either memorize or read very regularly)

Psalm 1	Psalm 8	Psalm 23
Psalm 2	Psalm 19	Psalm 27
Psalm 34	Psalm 150	1Corinthians 11:23-26
Psalm 91	Matthew 6:9b-13	1Corinthians 13
Psalm 100	Matthew 24: 3-31	Ephesians 6:10-18
Psalm 121	John 1:1-14	Philippians 2:1-16
Psalm 133	John 3:1-8, 16-21	Hebrews 11
	John 15	James 3

Sample Review System

The following is a basic plan of how you can review the suggested memorization verses included in this book over a 30-day period. This review system is only a suggestion and can be adapted, modified, or substituted with whatever system works for you.

*DAY 1	Day 2	Day 3
Eternally Saved through ONE Sacrifice: Jesus 1Corinthians 11:23-26	Grace Replaces the Old Law	Being Born Again
*DAY4	***DAY 5**	**Day 6**
The Spirit of Truth and the Power of God Psalm 19	Jesus is the Word of God – The Creator Psalm 2	Obedience is the Key–Faith without Works is Dead

XVI. MEMORY VERSES

*DAY 7	*Day 8	*DAY 9
Faith –the Only Way to Please God Psalm 1	Believers are Given the Full Authority of Christ	PRAYER: The Believer's Direct Line to God Hearing from God
*Day 10	*Day 11	*Day 12
Praising and Worshiping God John 3:1-8, 16-21	What it means to be a Christian Disciple Psalm 91	The Christian's Relationship to the World Psalm 121
*DAY 13	*Day 14	*Day 15
Psalm 100 Philippians 2:1-16	Raising Children is "Discipling" Psalm 34 A Surrendered Life (not My Will)	Christians must Bear Fruit Ephesians 6:10-18
*Day 16	*Day 17	*Day 18
How to be "More than Conquerors" Be "On Guard"	YOU can be Healed Too! 1Corinthians 13	Authority to Heal the Sick, Cast out Demons, Raise the Dead, Cleanse the Leper
*Day 19	*Day 20	*DAY 21
Persecution for Christ's Sake	The Christian's Love for the World Psalm 27	The Great Commission Psalm 8
*DAY 22	*DAY 23	*DAY 24
Unity amongst Believers Psalm 133	Pride Other Special Verses Psalm 23	Promises of Blessings John 1:1-14

XVI. MEMORY VERSES

*DAY 25	*DAY 26	*DAY 27
Stewardship and Integrity Giving The Power of Our Words Bitterness vs Forgiveness	Depend on His Strength and Power James 3 Ephesians 6:10-18	Claim God's Protection Peace that passes all Understanding God Promises Comfort in Tribulation Psalm 150
*DAY 28 John 15 Matthew 24:3-31 Hebrews 11		